# THRIVE

Prov. 11 : 28

Don't just Survive, Thrive!

Lisa Torrey

Pereze 63

# THRIVE

LIVE
LIKE
YOU
MATTER

## LISA TONEY

*Abingdon Press*
*NASHVILLE*

# THRIVE

## LIVE LIKE YOU MATTER

### Library of Congress Cataloging-in-Publication Data

Toney, Lisa.
  Thrive : live like you matter / Lisa Toney.
    pages cm
  ISBN 978-1-4267-5696-2 (binding: soft black, pbk. : alk. paper) 1. Self-actualization (Psychology) I. Title.
  BF637.S4T647 2013
  158—dc23

                                                                2013011497

13 14 15 16 17 18 19 20 21 22—10 9 8 7 6 5 4 3 2 1
MANUFACTURED IN THE UNITED STATES OF AMERICA

For my thrive team.

Love you guys!

Mom and Dad.

Jessica and Julie. Evamarie.

Denise and Tamiko.

Zoe, Gus, and Pax.

Carl, my faithful man.

Jesus, the thrive master.

Thank you for helping me thrive.

# CONTENTS

*Tell me, what is it you plan to do*
*with your one wild and precious life?*
—Mary Oliver


CHAPTER 1

# BURIED TREASURE

*The Wisdom of an Ancient Proverb*


W ELCOME TO THE PLANET. I'm glad you could
make it.

When you were born, you were given this time and place
to be alive. You have made it this far. Congratulations. The
question is, now what? What will you do with this one life
you have been given? How will you make the most of it?
How will you make a difference? How will you thrive?

You did not just fall out of the sky. The stork really did
not drop you off at your parents' front steps. You were created with purpose and intentionality. God wants you to be
here in this time and place as part of the seven billion people

who fill our planet. Even if you have never felt as if anyone wanted you, God does. God created you. God breathed life into you. God does want you to be here. God wants you to have this amazing life where you live life to the fullest and experience the wonder of the human existence through the relationships that you have. God wants you to thrive.

A life that thrives can impact our planet by leaving a legacy of goodness and generosity. A life that thrives has the ability to benefit others as well as find personal satisfaction. Doesn't that sound good? I'm in.

How do we get there, though? How do we thrive? Good questions. It always seems like something that happens to someone else, doesn't it? Yet this discovery of a life with meaning and purpose can be yours too. It is as thrilling as lifting the lid off a treasure chest. Are you ready to go treasure hunting?

I grew up in Michigan, so just finding the ground again after a snowy winter was like discovering buried treasure. But at the little lake near my childhood home, summer provided the best opportunities for treasure hunting. The water was so transparent, my two sisters, friends, and I could see minnows swim by our feet. We plucked them out of the water, staring eyeball to bulging fish eyeball as they squirmed and wiggled to escape our grip. The tiny hidden crayfish that peeked out from the shadows of docks and boat hoists were our dire enemies; those pinchers morphed in my mind into giant lobster-sized claws that could attack at any moment.

The clams were our treasure. They burrowed into the sand, often hidden with only slivers of their shells visible. But they did not hide as well as they thought. They left clam tracks—little lines drawn in the sand as they dragged their shells along the bottom of the lake. They snuggled down in the sand, tantalizing us in our search.

In our mighty sailing vessel—my dad's rowboat equipped with oars twice our size, a bucket of water, and a giant fishing net hanging from a pole—we cast off and followed clam trails, leaned over the edge of the boat, dug into the sand, and cast out our net. As those little clams emerged from the waters into our net, we piled them into our bucket of water and whooped with excitement. Again and again, one clam at a time, we searched, dug, and rejoiced. What a rush for a ten-year-old sailing the "high seas" in two feet of water.

With our bucket overflowing with treasure, we carried our hoard to the end of the dock. After counting our haul, we cast them back into their sparkling aquatic home so we could chase them again. Sure, they had all night to get a head start, but we'd be back. They could run—or crawl—but we would find them again. Half the fun was the search and, of course, the big net.

But the real thrill was definitely the treasure. On one of those perfect summer days, my dad decided to let us keep our bucket of treasure. Sitting on the dock, he opened up all those tiny clams with a knife and put all those pieces of clam meat in a pile. Back in the kitchen, my mom kept a watchful eye as my dad turned our treasure into homemade clam chowder.

As we set the picnic table with bowls and spoons, we were ready to dive into our delicious fresh catch. I slurped a creamy spoonful. Creamy and . . . gritty. I could taste sand in every bite. This story would have been way better if the clam chowder had been amazing, right?

## FINDING TREASURE IN A PROVERB

Searching for buried treasure is exhilarating; there's the potential of a mystery solved. Everyone I know loves a good treasure hunt, especially if the pursuit uncovers something rare of great worth.

That was how I felt when I first found a little life gem. It had always been sitting there, just waiting to be discovered . . . buried treasure. This time, though, it was a treasure I wanted to hold on to, not throw back. It was not an ingredient of sand soup. Instead, it shone like a valuable gold nugget.

This treasure was hidden in an ancient Hebrew proverb, a simple saying packed with truth. Although it has existed for many years, it positioned itself differently for me one day.

I was developing a spiritual coaching program, and I stumbled across this treasure as I was looking for a way to adequately describe the amazing changes I saw taking place when people lived with purpose and focus. As we matched spiritual life coaches with their mentees, I saw the power of intentional relationships to spark growth and hope. These purposeful relationships were helping people thrive.

As I reflected on the people who had invested in me, I noted so many who had intentionally poured time and wisdom into my life, thereby helping set me on a thriving course. As a child, I had parents who cherished and guided me. As a deeply depressed teenager who felt betrayed by a dear friend, I found healing through the care and nurturing guidance of a local pastor. As a cynical college student, I had the unwavering relational commitment of an unexpected kindred spirit who restored my faith in friendship. As a young professional, I benefited from a supervisor who offered wise counsel and direction. As a newlywed, I met weekly with a respected friend for advice and encouragement. When the parenting adventure began, the wisdom and experience of my older sister and parenting friends became priceless. The list goes on and on of people who devoted themselves to invest in me. Each offered me healing, direction, and wisdom.

Something significant happens when people invest in another life in a positive way. It can change the entire course of that person's future.

As I reflected on my experience and heard more stories of growth, healing, and hope from the spiritual coaching program, I searched for a word to communicate this way of life. I felt as if I were on a treasure hunt.

One day at home, as I flipped through the pages of my Bible, this proverb with the word *thrive* seemed to jump off the page. It shouted exactly what was happening in these relationships—successful living with health and balance. Then I looked at the entire phrase encompassing the word, and the idea rang true. This profound statement, just waiting to be discovered and put into practice, zeros in on the human capacity to *thrive:*

"Those who trust in their *riches* will F

A

L

L,

but the *righteous* will thrive like a green leaf."

Who doesn't want to thrive? We all want that for ourselves, our families, our businesses, and our friends. Thriving means you are doing life well.

This proverb is attributed to Solomon, an ancient king of Israel who was renowned for his good judgment. He had the ability to accurately assess a situation and make helpful and accurate decisions.

In the midst of a hotly debated custody battle, King Solomon offered an extraordinary solution. While accusations flew and emotions ran high between two women asserting parental rights, King Solomon suggested the baby be cut in two so that each woman could have half the child. A solution bordering on the barbaric was enough to prompt the real mother to immediately relinquish the child to the other woman rather than see her baby harmed. King Solomon affirmed that woman as the true mother because of her selfless love. The baby, still in one piece, was returned to her care.

People came from near and far to hear Solomon's wisdom. Even the famed Queen of Sheba from Ethiopia and Yemen decided to set out to meet King Solomon and personally assess this wisdom. She brought some of the riches of her kingdom. Would his wisdom be an equal trade? Solomon insightfully answered her questions, and she admitted, "The report I heard in my own country about your achievements and your wisdom is true. But I did not believe these things until I came and saw with my own eyes. Indeed, not even half was told me."

Solomon's proverbs were collected to offer wisdom to whoever could benefit from them. Royalty and commoners alike were permitted access to this gift of wisdom given to Solomon by God.

So, is it possible that an idea written by a respected leader thousands of years ago still holds valuable truth for us today? This book honors this one little jewel of a sentence, buried treasure, which speaks about what it means for a person to thrive.

Solomon captured a truth about our ability to thrive. When we trust in riches—things like possessions and money—we will not flourish or grow. We will fall, like a leaf, off a tree. Riches may create a gust of fun around us for a while, but during high winds, even more leaves end up falling off trees.

In writings attributed to an older King Solomon, he said, "There is nothing new under the sun." The pursuit of riches and the accumulation of possessions have apparently been desires of humanity for a really long time. Even nearly three thousand years ago, people trusted their lives to what they *had* rather than invest in who they were or what they could contribute to the planet.

The pursuit of riches may be fast and furious, but it doesn't fulfill the purpose for which we were created. If you have ever survived the stampedes of Black Friday, immediately following our day of thankfulness, you know our love of stuff is alive and well. With this false pursuit, in the end, life can come crashing down, falling all around us. When King Solomon shifted his focus to his riches rather than righteousness, his own proverb crashed down upon him as he lost much of his wealth, power, and status.

According to this proverb, trusting in riches may make you fall like a dead leaf, but there is something that will lead you to thrive like a green leaf.

I love putting new plants in the garden because I cannot wait to see their transformation from small green seedling to bountiful food-giving plant. What a thrill to find a plant covered in juicy red tomatoes or to discover a cascade of fresh berries bursting forth from the plant. My urban garden attempts to sprinkle the slight land space with bushes and vines that offer fresh produce throughout most of the year. Grapevines wind their way up our property border wall. Raspberry vines fill tight corners. Green bean and tomato vines climb in a small side garden next to our house. In tight spaces amidst a whole lot of cement and brick a healthy green plant peeks out, which one day will explode with delicious veggies or fruit.

Unfortunately, I am not a very competent gardener on my own. I require a team approach to growing most things. I put the plants in the ground and let God take over. Then I hope they survive and grow. Occasionally it works! Other times things start turning brown and funky. Sometimes there are bugs and fungus and mildew. The garden reminds me that hardly ever do things thrive without intentionality. Plants will not thrive without water, sun, weeding, fertilizing, and care. Neither will we.

## THE TREASURE OF RIGHT RELATIONSHIPS

This treasure of a proverb proclaims that there *is* something that will actually cause a life to thrive. It's being *righteous.*

You probably haven't said that word today yet. Go ahead, say the word out loud. Move it around in your mouth. Roll your *r.*

We don't use the word *righteous* much anymore. This is part of our treasure hunt, discovering this word either for the first time or all over again. Let's dust it off and hold on to it for a bit. It might just be treasure.

Back in 1962 the word *righteous* was huge. Bill Medley and Bobby Hatfield gave it fame as they adopted it as their stage name as the Righteous Brothers. I'd like to think they were intentional about this name. But the story goes that they adopted it after performing in a Los Angeles bar where a member of the crowd shouted, "That was righteous, brothers!" The name stuck. It was a moment of genius—or maybe a bit of fermented brew—that launched them and the word *righteous* into celebrity.

The Righteous Brothers might not have been saints, but they sang great songs like "Unchained Melody" and "You've Lost That Lovin' Feelin'."

> Oh, my love, my darling,
> I've hungered for your touch . . .

> You've lost that lovin' feelin',
> Whoa, that lovin' feelin' . . .

OK, back to business. This wise ancient proverb has more to offer us than a great band name. So let's spend some time with it and unearth this gem for our lives.

Solomon said those who were righteous would thrive. So what does it mean to be righteous? The Hebrew term *tzadik* (pronounced *tseh-dek*) means "righteous," and the Hebrew term *tzedakah* (pronounced *tzeh-daw-kah*) means "righteousness." *Righteous* and *righteousness* describe good relationships in terms of our words and actions. This is good living that treats people and situations honestly and displays integrity and care.

*Righteousness* encompasses our whole existence because who we are is mostly defined by our relationships in our families, workplaces, neighborhoods, places of worship, and more.

Righteous living does not just happen. You are not born righteous. Righteousness is intentional and takes constant interaction with your relational community. A life of righteousness requires investment not of money but of time and energy spent wisely.

Righteousness means having your relationships in a right order. Your relationship with God is right. Your relationships with others are right. You are in a good relational place with others and with yourself. Righteousness can be understood most simply as *right relationships*. Jesus talked about these right relationships this way: love God, love people. This treasure of a proverb that we have unearthed reveals that right relationships—righteousness—are essential if you want to thrive.

In ancient cultures and even until recent centuries, life could not be separated from the relationships of the surrounding community. The entire village celebrated weddings for days, extended families lived together in the same house, and occupations were handed down from one generation to the next. Life was inseparable from your relational community.

Many of us today do not live in similar strong community environments, but we still share with them one central component: the human need for connection with others. Even in our Western culture where we value our independence, people thrive best when they are upheld by and uphold others in healthy relationships.

Good relationships take work. They take intentionality. Most of us have some difficult relationships. They are strained; they are hard; they are complicated. If this ancient wisdom about righteousness is true, then we are going to be stuck until we can get these relationships healthier. Is it worth it? Is it possible? Yes, it is.

Do you want to live life to the fullest and enjoy it to the max? Do you want to contribute to humanity and make your life count? Do you want to thrive? Only you can answer these questions. People who answer them and decide to pursue righteousness are walking down the road that leads to a life of meaning and purpose—*that* is good living.

When we begin to thrive, we are living up to our potential. Jesus' brother James put it this way: "Let perseverance finish its work so that you may be mature and complete, not lacking anything." Notice the word *complete*. This is an English translation of the Greek word *teleios* (pronounced *tel-e-i-os*). This word does not mean that you are done with life. Rather, it refers to fulfilling the purpose for which something or someone was designed. A child who grows to be an adult is accomplishing *teleios*. A boat that has been built and sails the seas is reaching *teleios*. A garden that is planted, grows, and is harvested is fulfilling *teleios*. A buried treasure that is found is *teleios*. It is completing that for which you were created.

To thrive in life is to be *teleios*. It is to have the sense that we are doing what God intended for us to do with our lives.

Life rarely turns out the way we envision it. The beauty of being human and having free will is that we get to make choices constantly. These choices can lead to both rewarding and hurtful relationships. As I talk with people who are seeking to thrive, I hear many stories of loneliness, anger, or disappointment that have left deep wounds that seem to get in the way. Often the hurts of life prevent us from thriving as we desire.

Yet there are always those people who are able to do so. Life does not defeat them. What do they know about thriving in spite of their circumstances?

## A MAP FOR OUR TREASURE HUNT

Life on earth this side of heaven will never be perfect. But it can still be fulfilling. The chapters that follow zero in on character traits that will help you thrive in your relationships. These are life qualities that will encourage you to be a person who pursues right relationships, the righteousness highlighted in Solomon's proverb. Every relational encounter moves us closer to or further from thriving.

Not long ago I put six plants on the checkout counter at the store, but the clerk thought there were only five and charged me for that amount. Awesome! Is that her mistake or my responsibility? Probably both. I chose to tell her there were six plants so she would not get in trouble. Her appreciation was rather underwhelming since I was trying to save her bacon. Nonetheless, this minor moment that could have gone unnoticed was corrected. In chapter 2 we look at integrity. Sometimes we think only the big decisions matter or maybe the ones that involve others, but the small stuff adds up. Who are you when no one is looking? Your level of integrity reveals whether you are trustworthy in relationships, your *righteousness*.

In chapter 3 we springboard to the issue of boundaries. My first job as a lifeguard was at a youth event in northern Michigan in the middle of winter. The pool was inside and heated, but the fun for all the teenagers was running out into the cold snow, rolling in it, and then running back to the pool. It was a creative take on a polar bear dive. I knew it was completely slippery and unsafe. Yet, as a newly trained lifeguard, it was hard for me to corral the group and say no to the escapades led by my mentor and friend. The boundaries were fuzzy, but boundaries are important around water and in relationships. Radiating from a healthy core of integrity are our decisions about our relationships.

In spite of healthy boundaries, we still hurt each other. Getting wounded can happen so quickly. I love to watch the boys at the school our kids attend race scooters at breakneck speed. They go fast and play hard. Inevitably there is a crash, complete with scraped knees, blood, dirt, and tears. Those crashes become stories easily retold, and the evidence of the wound is easily seen on the skin. In contrast, the wounds that we adults receive from relationships are not so easy to see or explain. Since healthy boundaries are not always practiced on both sides of a relationship, most of us bear relational scars. These wounds can run deep and distract us from moving forward. The pain pushes blinders up around our souls and prevents us from thriving. In chapter 4, we learn that forgiveness is the only way to heal these wounds.

Healed wounds can make you stronger and ready to tackle the next thing around the corner. In chapter 5 we pursue the idea of focusing on goals. When a puck finds its goal in a big game, hockey fans cheer with joy. As my toddlers sat at their first local hockey game, they were startled and excited when the stadium burst to life. The lights flashed, horns sounded, music played, and people stood yelling and clapping as an all-out celebration commenced for each goal scored. What took only moments to achieve in a game took players years of dedication and perseverance. You may not have a hockey stick in your hands and skates on your feet, but you, too, can face and accomplish goals in your life. Goals give us a direction and focus. They help us be intentional with our time and energy so that we can thrive.

Accomplishing a goal can breathe strength into our spirits. A personal achievement can inspire the kind of courage that life requires. And life is not for the faint of heart. We are surrounded by scenarios that could go wrong at any moment. A recent routine drive home led our car past an intersection we have navigated hundreds of times. Suddenly, crunched cars piled up and sat haphazardly as the sound of blaring sirens approached them. Gawking onlookers drove past, curious to see what had happened. *That could have been us*, they thought. All around us there are things to fear, and when we permit those fears to take hold of our life and control us, we can become paralyzed and not pursue the opportunities before us. Chapter 6 encourages us to rise up with courage and thrive past the fears.

Living with courage allows us to take a stand for the things of this world that are not right. Some injustices are blatant; for example, poverty is horrific and often readily identified. Yet many injustices hover just under the surface. Some things look fine until we get closer. For example, we buy candy bars almost unconsciously for a quick bite, a little

sugar. But there is a disturbing reality in the chocolate indus-
try. A majority of chocolate produced by big-name candy
industries is produced with cocoa harvested from plantations
that employ child slave labor. Children are kidnapped, sold,
enslaved, and tortured so that we can keep enjoying inexpensive chocolate. It seems impossible that something we enjoy
so much comes at the expense of the lives of others. Is this
OK? Who is going to stand up and say, "No, this is not OK"?
Chapter 7 focuses on how we can change our world when we
fight the injustices around us.

Fighting injustice and changing the world inspire hope
and offer a better future. Chapter 8 encourages us to pursue
hope because it often comes in unexpected places. I dropped
on the sidewalk a box of three hundred flyers that I was
attempting to deliver to a school while also juggling my baby.
Just as I was contemplating how I was going to manage picking up and balancing the box while carrying the baby, a
woman I did not know appeared out of nowhere and said,
"You have your hands full. Let me help." She took the box
from me and delivered it to the office. Hope sometimes happens in unexpected ways and places and allows us to move
forward in life, lessening our cynicism. Hope allows us to
thrive.

Hope also shows us how to use our resources wisely.
There is so much good that could be done if only we had
more time. Chapter 9 addresses pacing ourselves in life
since there is so much to do and only so much time in

which to accomplish a task. Have you ever found yourself guessing which line is moving the fastest? I had just chosen the line at the gas station that I thought would get me through the wait the quickest. The cars were all lined up. I was up next. As I eyed the glorious empty spot in front of me and put my car into drive, an infuriating minivan roared in and stole my spot. Waiting is hard enough, but time stolen is even worse. We all have the same amount of time each day. We cannot make time speed up or slow down. So learning to use time wisely and pace ourselves leads to a life that will thrive.

Chapter 10 brings the book to a close with the call to excellence. Most of us get by with being just "okay." Why not go that extra mile to make something shine? One of my favorite Facebook posts is a big sign that says, "Whatever you do, give 100%." Right behind it is a smaller sign that declares, "Unless you are giving blood." You cannot be excellent at everything, and that is OK. However, you can be excellent at something, even if it is making a killer grilled cheese sandwich. Finding and using the unique gift that God has given you will lead you to thrive and make an amazing contribution to this planet. Now that is good living. And this book is about learning to thrive. Go on the treasure hunt; dig deep into the gem of a life that is too amazing to bypass or waste. Don't you dare just survive. Be one out of the seven billion people on this planet who actually thrives.

## DISCUSSION QUESTIONS

1. When have you been on a treasure hunt? What treasure were you pursuing?
2. How would you explain this idea of righteous living?
3. What people have invested in your life?
4. Whose lives have you invested in?
5. What relationships do you have that are healthy? What makes them healthy?
6. What relationships are you in that are not healthy? How do they affect your life?
7. What are some ways that you would like to see your life thrive?

*If you knew how much work went into it,*
*you wouldn't call it genius.*
*—Michelangelo*

CHAPTER 2

# "AYE, AYE, CAPTAIN"

*The Power of an Honest Yes*

S AILING IS IN MY BLOOD. I grew up around sailboats. There is something amazing about flying across the water with the waves splashing alongside you as the sails harness the wind. It feels like freedom. In a small sailboat with only a captain and one crew member, every move you make either works with the wind or against it. It propels you forward or quickly gets you into trouble.

In sailing there is room for only one captain to call the shots. This was a hard lesson for me to learn when I was a teenager and *knew* that I was ready to be the captain. Despite my dad's obvious skills and leadership, I struggled to say yes to someone else when I wanted to captain my way.

Learning to sail in a small boat, though, is the quickest way to learn the power of the word *yes*. If you say no when you should have said yes, you flip over. If you say yes and do not act on it, you flip over. If you cannot agree on what the *yes* should be, you flip over. If you say yes when you should have said no, you flip over. Growing up on the water, we saw many people who said yes to water sports before they were ready. One day when I was still a teenager, my dad and I went out on a small sunfish for a sail. We soon saw another sailboat in trouble. We circled and watched them for a bit to see if they needed help. I was eager to dive in and help, but my dad held me back. He waited to see if they could right their sails on their own. As we got closer we could see a boy about twelve and his uncle bobbing in the water alongside their overturned sailboat. Neither wore a lifejacket. They were getting pounded by the wind and waves and could not get their boat righted.

The great thing about small sailboats is that they maneuver easily. I knew I could get their boat back up for them. As soon as my dad gave the OK, I dived off our boat and swam over to them as my dad circled us. It was my *Baywatch* moment; the theme song played as I got them back up and ready to sail safely. By saying yes at the right time, my dad allowed us to make the rescue. Sailing taught me valuable lessons in saying yes at the right time and experiencing the difference that it makes. If you abused your *yes*, you'd probably end up all wet.

The captain gives the directions of where to go and when to make the changes. The crew needs to be ready to react, repeat the orders, and respond, "Aye, aye, Captain." Isn't that a great way to respond? I love that. It is a strong *yes* with action.

It is easy to throw out an insincere *yes*. Admit it. You've said yes a time or two when you didn't really mean it just to get someone off your back or to get some affirmation. We've all done it. Yet when this becomes a way of life, we are set up to sink rather than thrive.

## TOO EASY WITH OUR WORDS

Our words are intricately linked to our personhood. What comes out of your mouth reflects your heart.

Often we doubt that words contain truth. And we seek to make our words sound good. Spin them. Offer the sound bite. Our communication shifts away from being understood to being manipulative for self-gain. Communication becomes what we can get rather than what we can give.

We hear about famous people who lie and get away with it. They hire spin doctors, talking heads, and image consultants. Much of our culture no longer values that the word *yes* really means yes.

Have you ever known someone who agrees to things too easily? The person's head nods faster than he or she can keep up with it, like a bobblehead doll. "Sure, I can do that." "Yes, I'm in." "Yep, I'll be there." "For sure, I'm all over that." It makes people feel *so* good when others agree with them. The emotional indulgence of being a "yes-head" provides the person with a false sense of approval; being a "yes-head" comes at great cost.

If you like to say yes to try to gain others' approval, either you will constantly be annoyed at yourself for over-committing, or everyone around you is going to be angry with you for misrepresenting your true self. A false *yes* is really a dressed-up *no*.

When my husband first asked me out, he took me to the Spaghetti Factory. We were in graduate school and broke. Even though I hate spaghetti (I know, who hates spaghetti?), I said yes when I should have said no because I wanted him to like me. I set myself up to eat a meal that I didn't enjoy and then had to fess up about it later as we were heading out for more spaghetti. Saying yes can be easy, a relief, or the path of least resistance—plus we believe we're pleasing people. We like to be liked. Nodding your head in agreement even when you don't agree gives you the sense of maintaining peace and being on someone's winning side. Have you ever had to vote for something by a show of hands? All of a sudden hands shoot up around you, and your hand steals up because you want to vote like everyone else does. We all want to be liked, but we forget that thriving means valuing trust over agreement.

Has someone ever agreed to meet you but then never showed up? As you wait, you wonder whether you have the time right. *Should I order coffee or wait? Should I leave? Should I reschedule or just pretend that I forgot as well?* Or how about someone agreeing to do something but not carrying through? You depended upon her to show up to help at an event, but she never made it. Or you planned on his part in the presentation, and he didn't come through. It's maddening. When an agreement is broken, trust erodes. You are leery of setting something up again, uncertain that the person will actually show up.

If you do not follow through or never planned to take action on your *yes*, then you are lying. Liar. Fraud. Phony. Fake.

## *YES* TO INTEGRITY IN RELATIONSHIP

Raising sails and casting off the lines to be freed into the wind are invigorating. Just as a sailboat needs wind to fill its sails, a life that thrives is filled with integrity. Your personal integrity defines how people view you. Integrity is consistency of character, which is priceless. It is something that only you can develop and guard. The Greek word *ethos* (pronounced *e-thos*) refers to the guiding beliefs that identify us.

The things we value combine to make up our individual character. Our word *ethic* comes from this Greek root.

We've all heard the line: character is who you are when no one is looking. Character with integrity is found when your *yes* has both a positive intent and a follow-through. *Yes* comes from the Old English adverb *ye*, which means "surely" and "so," thus "surely so." It is a strong statement of belief and intent. Our *yes* is a window into our integrity. Our verbal assent is our affirmation that something is going to happen on our end. It is a verbal contract that means we are aligning ourselves with a particular idea. Our *yes* means we are ready to go. We are willing to act. We are who we say we are. Yes, absolutely, yes.

Thriving involves saying yes to right and proper relationships, to righteous relationships. Right relationships require trust. And trust can be formed only if we are reliable people. Think about the people you trust. Why do you trust them? If you are like me, the people you trust have shown themselves to be in right relationship with you by the power of their *yes*. The integrity of their word has made a difference in your life. They have earned your respect.

I both trusted and respected my grandmother. Her *yes* involved remembering my important days, such as my birthday and my basketball games, and cheering me on at both. Her *yes* meant that she paid attention to the small things that meant a lot, such as always having my favorite cereal as a kid, Lucky Charms, on hand. She became someone I could completely depend upon. And I learned from her that respect and trust are character traits that cannot be bought. They must be earned.

Learning a true *yes* may be a brand-new way of communicating for you, of moving forward by carefully considering the consequences of a proposed action, agreement, or request. It means you're learning to say yes only when you think you can actually fulfill it and then set out to do so.

We may not have a better word that is as clear and helpful as *yes* to state purpose and agreement. *Uh-huh* does not do it, you know? *OK* is good. *Yep* works. But *yes* nails it. The power of your *yes* needs to be redeemed. When you thrive, you begin this language restoration project. A heart redemption mission is under way.

I don't know much about construction. When a trip to help build homes outside Atlanta, Georgia, was presented to our high school youth group, I'm not sure what I was thinking by signing up. I was put on a team to restore a dilapidated home of a kind older woman. My project was to construct new doors for her home. Who knew doors could be so complicated? If I had been left to my own devices, that poor woman would have been better off with her old doors. Thankfully, a competent and patient team leader taught me what to do.

Construction can tear down the old and replace it with the new. Your behaviors do the same work. You can construct a life of integrity. Your *yes* powerfully builds character when fulfilled with action. Integrity stands on honesty, reliability, and truthfulness. The friends you trust come through for you. Priceless, right? This book calls for you to be one of those friends. To thrive and, through your thriving, to help others thrive. When you inspire someone to become a person of integrity by modeling righteousness—the right relationship seen through truthfulness in communication—you thrive. That friend or colleague thrives.

## A *YES* CAN OPEN DOORS

Think about it. Someone said yes to you at some point and allowed you to learn what you know now. For me, it came through a job as a donut froster. (Yes, that job really does exist.) It was in the bakery of our small-town grocery store. I was filling in for a girl who had been in a car accident. It was a good thing I was just a fill-in because I was not very good at it. On the first day, the baker told me to get the frosting out, which I promptly attempted by pulling out the tubs and spilling them all over the floor. Later she told me to make more frosting, and I used the same vanilla mix (rather than the different flavor mixes) in all the flavors of frosting, thinking we would add the appropriate flavoring. I probably should have been fired as a donut froster, but my baker boss let me come back the next day and the next. She said yes to me, albeit out of desperation, and she gave me a chance. She invested in me, and I'll have you know, I became a rockin' donut froster.

Of course, timing is crucial in any relationship. We don't say yes all the time or to everyone. Right relationships are genuine and allow for disagreement and compromise. Strong relationships involve respect and care for others' opinions and beliefs, even if they are different from our own. Being a good friend does not mean we always say yes.

Relationships that thrive are those where there is honesty and respect for one another's opinions. There is room for each person to say no rather than an obligation to say yes. There is a capacity for compromise without relational consequences. Right relationships allow for interaction and negotiation. Authentic relationships show respect for each other's personhood.

If you do not have many authentic relationships, it is time to form some. The best way to do that is to become the kind of friend you would like to have. Be a person of your word. Follow through. Jesus put it this way: "All you need to say is simply 'Yes.'" Build your integrity. The good news is that you can develop integrity one step at a time; one honest decision after another leads to a life that is reliable. If you can be trusted, you are well on your way to living out that hidden treasure of righteousness. Trust enables a life of righteousness that will thrive.

We need to be wise with our *yes* but not stingy with it. A *yes* might begin a whole new adventure. Integrity makes a soul healthy, and it makes a culture healthy. It allows us to take people at their word. Change begins with us. What would it look like to become a people who could say what we mean and mean what we say? And hold our silence or speak considerately when needed? I tell my kids not to talk with their mouths full. Often as toddlers they are so excited to say something, they can hardly stand it. Half-eaten food falls out of their mouths as they try to get their words out. It's gross, and I can't understand them. When they do swallow before they speak, I can understand them, and I have far fewer messes to clean up. We should not say everything that we think. Holding our tongues is like taking a moment to swallow food. It gives us time to try a sentence before we spew it out there and make a mess that needs to be cleaned up.

We might have to say, "Let me get back to you on that" or "I'm not sure. I don't want to commit too soon. Let me think about it." In an age of instant gratification, perhaps we jump in with our words too quickly at times. This leads to a culture that promotes fast decisions and fast communication too often not based on careful thought. Practicing the pause is countercultural but can lead to a life filled with integrity so that we might thrive. We need to fulfill the *teleios*, the purpose, for which we were created. Become a person of immense integrity. Amaze people. Integrity will do that.

So how do you learn how to say yes at the right moments? We can't say yes all the time, nor should we. But saying yes with integrity can propel us forward to new adventures. It allows us to stretch and grow and participate in life. How do we do that? Find wise people, whom you trust, and ask them for advice. Or maybe someone who has walked the path before you could give you insight that you had not considered. Before saying yes or no for life's tough decisions, make a list of pros and cons. Think through the reality of what a *yes* would involve from you in time, money, and energy.

If you do not have enough resources to make a *yes* statement that you can back up, then wait. Do not commit to it. Gather resources. Find help. Read wisdom, such as the proverbs of our friend King Solomon. This might be just what you were looking for to make wise decisions.

Seek the wisest counsel of all. Take your questions to God, who is filled with infinite wisdom. Ask God if you should say yes to a particular situation. Wait for a peace in your soul as an affirmation from God. When you end a prayer with an "amen," you are saying, "And let it be so." It is a declaration of affirmation. It is a big yes, indeed. "Yes, I'm seeking God's wisdom on this life issue. I need direction. I need counsel. I need guidance with this one."

Having conversations with God is a great way to seek God's wisdom. Prayer is not only a way to process life but a way to keep your soul healthy. People cannot always be trusted, but God can. Investing in this relationship with the one who is completely trustworthy and wise can help you thrive. Just as fast as a thought can enter your head or heart, it can be reflected to God in a prayer. Prayer can happen anywhere and anytime; there are no right words or wrong words to use. You can express all emotions, experiences, and questions to God through prayer. God is big enough to handle it. After all, God created you as a complex emotional and relational being. God knows that it often takes us time and many conversations to work through issues. God gave prayer to us as a means to interact with God on a regular basis. It is soul therapy at its finest.

Prayer also allows us time to pause and listen to God's leading in our lives. Finding a place or time to stop the chaos of life so that we can hear the gentle whispers of the Divine is essential to maintaining a healthy relationship with God. I use my swim time at the gym to do this. Those pool prayers are when I have focused time to just talk and listen to God. Whether you are taking a shower, commuting to work, or carving out special time in your day, God is always available to you.

Being open to receiving wisdom from God can change the entire approach to a situation. God is amazing at providing a third alternative when you see only two approaches to a particular situation. When my husband had an opportunity for grad school in Illinois and I had a wonderful career opportunity in California, God opened the door for us to be able to do both things rather than have to choose one scenario. God loves to surprise us in ways that we never could anticipate, but to receive those treasures, we have to seek God's wisdom.

At the core, God is integrity filled. God is incapable of dishonesty or deceit. God will always tell the truth. That does not mean that God always gives us what we want or says what we want to hear. God sees things from a different perspective than we do.

## LEARNING TO SAY YES TO GOD

Learning to say yes to God opens a whole new approach to living. This is where "Aye, aye, Captain" becomes essential even if we have never been sailing. When God prompts our spirits to act or speak, we have a choice. God is not forceful. God knows it is much more meaningful if we choose to say yes on our own rather than be forced like a puppet on a string to react. Choice is important. Having a choice in life and having a choice with God are great things about being human. We have the opportunity to make good choices, have integrity, and say yes to things that count.

Learning to listen to God takes a quiet spirit, time, practice, and a willing heart. Saying yes to God takes courage. A *yes* to God means you trust your life to very capable hands. God once called me to get involved in leadership with the church. I honestly was not sure I wanted to do that. But God very clearly said to me that if I was not happy with the way things were in the church, I needed to be involved to make a difference. So I said yes to God and have been working to make things fun and relevant in the church since then.

God created you to thrive in this life. When God repeatedly presents you with an opportunity, it might be an invitation to say yes and thrive in the life you have been given.

God wants to see you thrive. You honor your Creator when you do the things that only you can do. Saying yes to God is a good way to put our proverb into practice. A right relationship with God is the foundation of righteous living.

God will pursue you out of love. God is often the hardest to say yes to because you often think that means you must say no to yourself. The reality is that a *yes* to God is going to lead to adventures that you never could have imagined on your own. God's got your back. Easy and complacent are not God's style. Having a *yes* lifestyle with God is often challenging. But that keeps you growing and moving forward in a way that allows you to thrive.

When you really mean yes, say it, and follow through. You will begin to thrive. People of integrity have a solid foundation for right relationships. You will begin to align yourself with righteous living. You will begin to get your relationships in right order because the people you interact with will begin to trust you. Others will know that they can count on you. People will want to be in relationship with you because they know they will get an honest answer from you.

*Yes* gets things done. *Yes* changes lives. It might even change yours.

# DISCUSSION QUESTIONS

1. Name people you know personally whom you consider to be full of integrity.
2. How can you build integrity in your life?
3. Share an occasion when someone let you down after having agreed to something.
4. Share an experience when you said yes to something that led to an opportunity you had not anticipated.
5. What is your experience with prayer?
6. How can you use your *yes* to help you thrive?

*Be who you are and say what you feel, because those who mind*
*don't matter and those who matter don't mind.*
—Bennett Cerf

CHAPTER 3

CONSTRUCTION &
EMOTICONS

*The Protection of a Thoughtful No*

I USED TO DO A LOT of driving for my job and considered the road a friend. My recruitment territory included four states in the Midwest, so I became very familiar with the roads in that area. While driving down the interstate in Indiana one beautiful fall day, I encountered the dreaded orange warning signs that strike fear into the heart of every commuter. The one word no one wants to see when you are behind the wheel. The one word that changes everything when on the road: *construction.*

I took a deep breath, slowed the car, and began to recalculate my morning plans. Soon, though, I realized this was not your normal construction zone. The roadside signs featured emoticons, with moods and facial expressions ☺. Rather than being purely informational or threatening fines, these construction signs encouraged frustrated drivers. Bad news was tempered with positive comments such as "You are almost through"; "Only a little bit more"; and "You are almost done."

The emoticon faces on the signs got progressively happier. It was the most polite construction zone I have driven through. I've never met with a construction site like that again, which makes me wonder if I was in an episode of the *Twilight Zone*. But the memory is vivid, which makes the site manager a genius. Those signs turned a negative experience positive. They turned a *no*—"No, you may not drive here the way you normally do"—into a somewhat enjoyable experience.

A typical construction site has strategically placed warning and caution signs. They tell you to slow down. They alert you to detours. These warning signs protect the drivers, the passengers, and the construction workers. However frustrating drivers find them, construction signs establish a safety boundary for passing vehicles. They indicate that people can get hurt and equipment damaged if drivers do not respond to them.

Similarly, in our relationships, a strong communication sign is thrown up when the word *no* is used in conversation.

Unfortunately, these communications are not accompanied by happy emoticons.

These modern iconography punctuations appear all over social media and even in print, but they do not show up to help us in a face-to-face conversation. Right relationships, the righteous living that we are pursuing, rely heavily upon open and sincere communication.

As soon as we become aware that we have a choice, we begin to exercise our voices to communicate our personal preferences. *This is what I do and do not like.* Having an opinion is important; it makes us individuals. Communicating that opinion with kindness and respect is an art. Since there are so many of us sharing the planet, we are bound to bump elbows. We step on each other's toes. We end up with broken hearts. We get beat up just being relational beings.

*No* is a word that serves us well, though. It protects us. *No* celebrates that we are beings with free wills who have a choice. We get to decide what we think is best for us. We get to choose how we want to live. *No* can be empowering and freeing.

Yet it doesn't always feel that way.

Saying yes feels more considerate and open. *No* excludes things. It draws boundaries. *No* rejects something.

Why do we need to talk about *no* if we want to thrive? There is a time when both *yes* and *no* accompanied with action, will make a big difference to who we are and how we live. The goal then, is to figure out when, where, why, and how to say these two small words that make a big impact.

## AN INAUSPICIOUS BEGINNING

From the very beginning of time, Adam and Eve were given the opportunity to say no. God placed them in a beautiful and lavish paradise, and they could eat anything they wanted except the fruit from one tree, the tree of the knowledge of good and evil. Adam and Eve were surrounded with beautiful and delicious fruit. To their right hung juicy mangoes, to their left grew sweet oranges, straight ahead were delicious bananas, and right behind them were scrumptious avocados. Maybe, too, apples, pears, pomegranates, persimmons, peaches, and plums. They lived in the world's first farmers' market. But desire got the best of them. Despite all the *yeses* of God, one *no* was just too tempting to resist. They became obsessed with getting the fruit from the tree they were forbidden to eat.

Ultimately, God was extending relational trust, not fruit. This offering was precious because it was the gift of choice. God is no puppet master. A *yes* to God is meaningful because it begins and maintains a relationship of obedience with the Creator. In contrast, a *no* (in this instance) becomes a rejection of God's discerning guidance. Adam and Eve could trust their friendship with God and choose to believe God.

Through that choice, they could know and enjoy an uncontaminated relationship with God and each other. In the end, however, the appeal of being godlike was too tempting for them. The power to know both sides of the story, good *and* evil, was too enticing.

They chose to begin a relationship with evil through the tempting wiles of a snake. Adam and Eve decided to say no to God rather than the snake, scarring their relationship with God. The relationship with the snake that spouted lies became a game changer. Humanity left the world of complete goodness and innocence behind. The world is now full of both good and evil.

Adam and Eve became obsessed with eating the fruit that was forbidden them. Like them, it is as if we are hardwired to want what we should not want and do what we should not do.

Saying no just feels good sometimes. It gives us a sense of power and control over our lives, our relationships. So we think. As much as God loves to give us choice, saying no to God does have consequences: after the first human *no*, the consequence was getting kicked out of Paradise.

We all have said yes when we should have said no. I waitressed my way through most of high school and college. My first waitress job was at a tiny family-run restaurant. There were six tables and the counter. The restaurant specialized in homemade pies and soups. I had a good relationship with my boss, and I liked the people I worked with. I enjoyed working there a lot, but a place down the street was rumored to pay twice as much money as I was making. So I quit my job and got hired at the place down the street. It was a classic case of trusting in riches rather than righteousness. I was miserable there. The restaurant was a greasy spoon, and my boss was creepy. I said yes to that job way too quickly and then found myself desperate to get out of it. Thankfully, God provided me with a lesson quickly learned and an even better third working alternative, but I definitely learned to be careful about saying no to good things.

There is always someone (a snake, for instance) who will try to convince us that there are ways to thrive that do not include a right relationship with God. But integrity and righteousness, right relationships, are God's idea and our choice to embrace.

## SAYING NO TO MANIPULATIONS

Jesus himself had to say no to the snake in order to thrive. Just like Adam and Eve, he found himself tempted. Three times Jesus responded with a resounding no when it would have been self-gratifying to say yes. Even when the ache of a forty-day fast filled his being, Jesus was still able to deny Satan's invitation to turn stones to bread so that Jesus could break his fast. The second temptation found Jesus perched on the heights of a ledge higher than any climbing wall. Satan offered him a display of power: if Jesus accepted it, he could walk away in one piece even though he cast himself over the edge. Again, Jesus said no to preserve his integrity and form a boundary around his power that excluded Satan. The final temptation was the offer for Jesus to become the most powerful ruler over all the nations. Jesus again said no and embraced the steadfast decision to love the world as a servant, not to walk as a tyrant. Proverbs 11:28 warns against trusting in the riches and accompanying powers of this world. Whatever you don't have, especially when others have it, can become a temptation. As desire sets in, it becomes easier to believe the hisses of a slithering snake than to say no and preserve a proper boundary.

In Jesus' firm *no* to these grand temptations, a pattern emerges that underlies a life that thrives. The pattern is built on the integrity of his *yes*. Jesus' priority was maintaining a relationship with God his Father. In doing this, he recognized the need to have a strong *no*. This *no* was essential to keeping his *yes* powerful. It allowed Jesus to set boundaries around his mission and his relationships with others and block out distractions. Jesus modeled the effects that a thoughtful *no* can have on one's life.

*No* is often difficult to say when there is the opportunity for easy personal gain. John Woolman, a Quaker retailer, itinerant preacher, and staunch abolitionist, made some tough business decisions based on conscience, not opportunity. He said, "It had been my general practice to buy and sell things really *useful*. Things that served chiefly to please the vain mind in people, I was not easy to trade in; seldom did it; and whenever I did I found it weakened me as a Christian."

These *noes* from Jesus and John Woolman served to establish their priorities in life. They said no to anything that would not help accomplish that mission. They said yes to everything that did accomplish that mission, and this concentration allowed them to thrive.

## THE *YES* BEHIND A *NO*

God's *no* is for our protection. Perhaps in the grand scheme of things, the timing may not be right. God may have other plans for us. There might be something better down the road. God gives well-boundaried noes with purpose. We may not know the mind of God, but we do know the heart of God.

God gave us *no* for a reason: to provide us with boundaries that help us thrive. In their book *Boundaries*, John Townsend and Henry Cloud write,

> Having clear boundaries is essential to a healthy, balanced lifestyle. A boundary is a personal property line that marks those things for which we are responsible. In other words, boundaries define who we are and who we are not. Boundaries impact all areas of our lives: Physical boundaries help us determine who may touch us and under what circumstances—Mental boundaries give us the freedom to

have our own thoughts and opinions—Emotional boundaries help us to deal with our own emotions and disengage
from the harmful, manipulative emotions of others—
Spiritual boundaries help us to distinguish God's will from
our own and give us renewed awe for our Creator—Often,
Christians focus so much on being loving and unselfish
that they forget their own limits and limitations.

Think of boundaries like a fence. A fence gives your property a sense of ownership and definition. A fence communicates
to the neighborhood that this space is mine, and the space outside is not. A fence keeps things protected and clearly delin-
eated. The things you value—your family, your house, your car,
your pets, your garden—are kept inside that boundary line.

City living is very different from where I grew up with no
fences. Urban dwellers like to contain wide open spaces with
boundary lines, maybe because space is at such a premium.
People are desperate to claim every last inch of property and
make it their own. In the city there are fences everywhere:
cement block walls, chain-link fences with barbed wire, brick
walls, green hedges, and wrought-iron gates. However, it is
often little more than a visual barrier for neighbors. On our
side, we can still smell our neighbors' barbecue and hear their
outdoor conversations, as I am sure they can ours.

The household goal isn't only to have a good fence but
also to protect, enjoy, and make good use of the yard.
Boundaries in life do the same thing. They help you enjoy
and cultivate the yard, which is your life.

Beyond physical boundaries, an emotional boundary allows you to say no when someone in your life does not speak or act appropriately. Establishing a guideline for people who do not live the same way that you do can be crucial to your well-being.

I am allergic to most cats and dogs. I love dogs but not dog hair. When we have friends or family visit us and they bring their animals, we ask that they not allow them in the house. It would be easy for me to say yes for the sake of being harmonious. That *yes* would sound nice initially, but I would become bitter and resentful while struggling with allergies instead of enjoying the company of people I care about. Boundaries help you communicate honestly. They help you thrive.

## THE HUMAN CHALLENGE

Yes, it is a tough day when the realization sets in that you're not a god or a superhero; you are just human. It can also be a wonderful day when things start to change in your life and you realize that you have been given simple tools: the *yes* and the *no*. In order to care for yourself and your relationships, you begin to set boundaries by saying no to things that do not breathe life and health into your relationships.

You are a wonderfully made human being. You are smart. You are capable. You are amazing. And you are called to set limits to protect those gifts of being human. Boundaries help you to function within those limits. You need to work out and work through a system of priorities in order to thrive.

Orville and Wilbur Wright were committed to the priority of creating a plane that could fly. These brothers battled depression and family illness and eventually started a bicycle shop that would begin their experiments in flight. People laughed at and mocked them for their attempts, but they persevered. After several years of hard work and many failed prototypes, the Wright brothers finally went airborne. They were able to build a plane that flew in the sky and stayed there. Their priority was to fly regardless of who told them no. Despite the discouragement, they focused with precision on the dream that allowed them to thrive.

Being able to draw lines that create boundaries around what's important helps you navigate responses to the constant array of opportunities:

What will you do with your time?

What relationships will you invest in?

What will you eat, and when will you exercise?

How will you spend money?

How will you attend to and protect your sexuality?

How will you nourish your spirit?

There are so many opportunities around us that we are constantly being bombarded with questions that demand a yes-or-no response either with our words or our actions.

Don't know where to begin to discern priorities? For starters, look at your bank account and your day planner. The way you spend your time and money speaks about what is important to you. If you don't like what you see, set new priorities. Life gets crowded too quickly. If you don't set your priorities, others will set them for you. Are you investing in the things and people that you love? If not, then you need to fight for those things and those people. Say no to the things that interfere with spending your time and money on them.

Author and nationally syndicated radio show host Dave Ramsey exerts a significant countercultural force in our society, helping create financial boundaries and establish priorities. Ramsey billboards call us to "Act Your Wage," reminding us to spend only what we have rather than spending on credit, and help many recover a financial *no*! If we can learn to say no with our words and actions financially, then our *yeses* will be much more enjoyable and affordable!

## MASTERING THE ART OF SAYING NO

Just in case this is a new word for you, go ahead and say it out loud: "No."

I know. It probably feels strange on your lips.

It's OK.

You'll adjust.

Have you ever met someone who can say no so well that you walk away from the conversation thinking the refusal was your idea in the first place? It is a bit confusing. What just happened? It is rare to see this gift of communication in action. These people understand that hearing no is painful, and thus, they have found creative ways to redirect or reaffirm other areas in the midst of saying no.

I asked someone to come over to our house and help me with a project. He was too busy to do so, but he responded with, "Thank you for the opportunity. I would be happy to do that sometime next week. However, I cannot this week." He basically told me no. But he did it kindly and encouraged me in the process.

Learning to master the art of saying no in a way that takes some of the stinger out of the wound is a helpful discipline that will allow you to thrive in your relationships. Learning to decline with kindness builds character because it requires self-control.

It is much easier for people to hear no when there is some love in the mix—what the Scriptures call "speaking the truth in love." So how do you do it?

When you need to tell someone no, try using this approach. Begin the conversation by affirming the person or the request: "Thank you for . . ." or "You've done a good job at . . ." Put the difficult area of communication in the middle: "Unfortunately, I cannot . . ." or "I know you didn't want to have me say no to this, but I need to . . ." Also, ending the conversation on a note of loving-kindness is fitting: "Thank you so much for thinking of me"; "You are so good at reaching out to people. I know you'll find an amazing replacement."

I call this approach *a communication love sandwich*. A communication love sandwich can make interactions healthy and provide positive experiences, even when there are difficult things to be said. Saying no does not have to wound someone or be impossible to get out of your mouth. People appreciate honesty and clarity. If you beat around the bush, there will just be confusion. Is someone going to show up before the meeting on Thursday to set up the meeting room? *Hmm. Well, I think so, but I'm not positive.* This response leaves the question unanswered. When you communicate with clarity and compassion, you can provide a resource to help get something done.

In contrast, if you nail the issue quickly and firmly but without kindness, you will likely wound. Kindness and clarity are a great combination. When you communicate by affirming rather than throwing barbs and wounding others, you are beginning to find success in your communication. You are beginning to find the tools for right relationships and understanding how "the righteous will thrive."

## THE ART OF HEARING NO

Learning to graciously receive the word *no* is another art. Tensions can run high when we hear a negative response, even expressed in the kindest manner. Becoming defensive is a natural tendency. One of the best things you can do when you are told no is to pause before you react.

I applied for a job in college in the admissions office along with a few of my friends. They got hired; I did not. I still remember them excitedly sharing their acceptance letters with our dorm mates. Hearing them, I just wanted to hide in my dorm room and not come out—ever. I thought of every reason on the planet that *I* should have been hired over them. In the middle of my sadness, I was defensive. It was hard enough to be told no, to be rejected, but then having to tell my friends I did not get the position amidst their joy was agony. It took me time to frame that situation and realize that hearing a *no* to something meant there likely would be a *yes* down the road somewhere else.

Think of receiving difficult news as an opportunity to discover alternatives that you have not previously considered. Thomas Edison tested more than three thousand filaments before he came up with his version of a practical lightbulb. That was three thousand times he got a *no* thrown at him. Yet Edison did not allow himself to be discouraged and give up. He learned by testing and moved forward with determination. Edison said, "If I find 10,000 ways something won't work, I haven't failed. I am not discouraged, because every wrong attempt discarded is another step forward."

John Grisham began his career as a lawyer who loved to write. His first book took him three years to write. *A Time to Kill* was rejected twenty-eight times before a publisher decided to print it for a five-thousand-copy run. Now, his books have sold more than 275 million copies. Giving up because someone has told you no will not lead you to thrive. But making changes, adapting, and pressing on will. Yes, sometimes people will tell you no to be spiteful. But usually it is with a good reason. You have the choice to learn from the experience and an opportunity to ask questions. Why did they say no? Would they have said yes if something was different? What are they looking for? Is it something that I can change? This is a good time to be self-reflective and consider how it can lead to personal growth.

Thriving people seek those in their lives who can speak a gracious and life-affirming *no*. It means you have people who can tell you the truth. Hearing no also builds character. If you had gotten an initial *yes*, you might not have relied on your creativity to try a new approach.

When we were faced with tough budget cutbacks at church, our staff heard no a lot when we needed funding. Our team learned to be focused and disciplined in using our budget money sparingly. We found ways to cut the budget. We used to take all our linens to the dry cleaner after big events, but we decided to ask for volunteers with the spiritual gift of laundry. Amazingly, a wonderful group stepped forward. Not only were we able to save money, but we also allowed people to serve the local church with a job they could do that brought them joy.

Being rejected in a job, for an idea, or in a relationship can be hard. When we are invested, a *no* feels very personal. However, if we are able to receive a *no* as gracefully as possible, evaluate it, and then move on, we are on the road to thriving.

## PRACTICAL POINTERS

Using two little words effectively—*yes* and *no*—can transform your life. Here are tools to help you be effective and thrive in your responses:

*Evaluate the situation* in terms of pros and cons. What are some likely outcomes if you say yes or no? Do you have the information you need to make a wise decision?

*Consult.* Identify a few spiritually mature people who might have gone through a similar situation. Do they advise a *yes* or *no* response? If you trust them to speak into your life, carefully consider their counsel.

*Consider the consequences.*

In terms of time commitment, do you have enough time to follow through on your decision?

If the question is financial, do you have enough money to say yes to this? If you do not have the money, you should probably say no. What will it cost you later if you say no? What will it cost you later if you do not say no?

In terms of relational impact, whose lives will be altered or influenced by your *no*? Are they in agreement with you?

Do you have their support? How will this affect your relationships with family, friends, neighbors, coworkers, and others?

How will this decision impact one or more of your life priorities? Can you implement healthy relational boundaries? What are the possible results of this decision?

*Pray and read Scripture.* Talk to God about this decision that needs to be made, and ask for guidance. Maybe you are sensing a *yes* or *no* deep within your spirit. Listening for God's voice means you need to find space for some quiet in your life.

Does your decision align with Scripture? In the classic *The Christian's Secret of a Happy Life*, Hannah Whitall Smith addresses a relationship between our inner impressions, feelings, or what she calls "leadings": "It is essential . . . that our 'leadings' should all be tested by the teaching of Scripture. But this alone is not enough. They must be tested as well by our own spiritually enlightened judgment, or what is familiarly called 'common sense.'"

*Sleep on it.* Seriously. Sleep before you act. Perspective is an amazing thing. A night of sleep can change everything. You have fresh eyes, more energy, less emotion, and the advantage of living with your decision for twenty-four hours before you act on it.

## STAYING ON THE ROAD

There is no fail-safe plan for making great decisions all the time. Sometimes we just make the wrong one. When we do, we have to get back up and try again. We fix what we can fix. We apologize for saying something stupid, and we move on. We can't afford to be paralyzed by a wrong decision. Sometimes we say yes when we should have said no, and sometimes we say no when we should have said yes. You are not perfect. Neither am I. Nevertheless, we can give it our best shot.

Are you ready to go with your *no*? You can do it. Just don't say no when you should say yes. Say yes more than you say no. But please, say something. You are a created, intelligent, amazing, capable human being designed to thrive in the life you were given. As Jesus declared, "All you need to say is simply 'Yes' or 'No.'" And thrive.☺

## DISCUSSION QUESTIONS

1. When has someone said no to you in a way that was hurtful?
2. When have you said no to someone and hurt him or her with that response?
3. Who do you struggle to say no to? Why?
4. What do you struggle to say no to? Why?
5. To what situation do you think you could apply the "love sandwich"?
6. What are some of your top priorities?
7. What boundaries do you need to draw around these priorities to protect them?

*Resentment is like drinking poison and expecting*
*the other person to die.*
—Carrie Fisher

CHAPTER 4

SPLINTERS

*The Relief of a Pulled Barb*

YOU NONCHALANTLY RUN YOUR HAND along
a piece of wood. Then, *BAM*, pain shoots through
your hand. A splinter. How does something so small hurt so
badly? Have you ever had to remove a splinter from the hand
of a child? My kids like to run on their grandparents'
wooden dock. Despite the mantra of "walk, slow down,
don't run," there is the inevitable crash, and a shard or set of
wood shards jut out of my child's flesh. It is quite a process
to remove the splinters from a squirming child afraid of pain.
Get out the peroxide. Bust out the needle from the sewing kit.
Dig out the tweezers from the medicine cabinet. Grab the ice

pack. The Sesame Street Band-Aid. Inflicting pain upon a child is the worst. You know it's for his or her ultimate good because the splinter will get infected if you don't get it out. But there is no Splinter Removal Fairy. Only the pain of the process.

Our family didn't camp often, but the experience provided memorable moments with my parents and two amazing sisters. We never went far from home, since in the abundance of trees and lakes of the northern peninsula of Michigan there was plenty to see. All five of us would set off in a friend's borrowed camper to take in the sights and have adventures along the way. My mom fried apples we picked from a wild apple tree. We jumped the rocks over cold freshwater streams. We hiked the paths of state parks to find hidden waterfalls. And there's nothing like outdoor bonfires, roasted marshmallows, and scorched long hair. (Yes, there was a reason we didn't camp often.)

One time when we were visiting the magnificent Tahquamenon Falls, we climbed the steps and were kept safe by the wooden guide rails along the perimeter of the steps and falls. They might have kept us safe from falling, but my older sister, maybe nine years old at the time, ran her hand along a railing and got a deep splinter. My dad was the hero who painstakingly removed it while my mom held her tightly.

Although a splinter is a physical barb in your flesh that can usually be removed easily, splinters aren't so straightforward in our relationships. The quest for righteousness, that is, right relationships, is a messy process. Right relationships take a lot of work. We rarely say what we mean. Our communication can be lazy. Our listening skills are untrained. Arguments ensue. Fights break out. Resentments form. Relationships are broken. The shards that fly from an argument get lodged in our souls. Harsh words land in our hearts and cause our souls to ache. Like porcupine quills, they can work toward our hearts and be deadly. Bitterness builds, festers, and infects relationships.

Why do we hurt each other so easily? French writer Marquis de Vauvenargues wrote, "Emotions have taught mankind to reason." The balance of emotion and reason allows us to live life to the fullest. Even though our reason and emotions often war with each other, they are great blessings that enrich our existence.

However, there is a shadow side to these two human qualities. We use them to think and feel most strongly about ourselves, for we are our own constant companions. We defend ourselves and our needs. We know what we like and what we do not like. This becomes the challenge of living together on one planet. All seven billion of us (and counting) think and feel differently.

About everything.

All the time.

That causes friction.

All the time.

About everything.

All the time.

To thrive, we have to get the splinters out. Seriously, there is no alternative, so don't even think about skipping this chapter.

The good news is that you are not alone. We are all in this splinter removal project together.

## WHO'S GOT THE PROBLEM?

Jesus began this splinter removal project thousands of years ago. Even in his day shards got thrown around, wounding people left and right. Jesus asked poignant questions dealing with forgiveness in his famous Sermon on the Mount: "Why do you look at the speck of sawdust in your brother's eye and pay no attention to the plank in your own eye? How can you say to your brother, 'Let me take the speck out of your eye,' when all the time there is a plank in your own eye?"

Jesus, in his genius, calls attention to the fact that it is much easier for us to complain about being offended by others than it is for us to change our offensive behavior. The plank seems to be the obvious choice to remove first, but we leave it there to focus on someone else. It seems absurd to think that you could wander around with a plank jutting out of your eyeball and have no one notice.

It is far easier to point out the faults in others: they were rude; they were wrong; they lied; they were manipulative; they cheated; they got angry; they hurt me. These things may all be true. There are so many ways we hurt one another, sometimes on purpose and often without even knowing it. Jesus calls us to make sure that we are doing a regular self-inventory before we address all the *they dids*. He calls us to examine our own motives, words, and behaviors to determine whether we need to remove something in our own lives. Perhaps our selfish nature clouds our vision.

Just tonight my words failed to be as kind with my family as they should have been. The people we love the most sometimes get the brunt of splintering. I cannot take my words back, but I can apologize and try to do things differently tomorrow.

Self-reflection requires you to admit you are wrong about some things. It might mean you have to change. At the very least it might cause you pain. So perhaps it is best to avoid it. Hide from the hurt. Ignore the wounds to your soul. Yet if you want to thrive, you have soul surgery to do. Splinters need to be removed. This means addressing the times, places, and people that have wounded you. Introspection and reflection—shining a light on your words and actions that were contributing factors—require courage. But that is how you learn and grow. With honest evaluation of the situation—what you contributed, what others contributed, and what you can do to change—there is hope for pulling out those splinters.

Why do the splinter removal surgery? Life and freedom. You will be free to find righteousness (right relationship with others and with God). Free to thrive.

This splinter removal project might be one of the most significant things you ever do. It is one of the most radical opportunities for transformation for someone who wants to practice right relationships in a healthy and life-giving way. Jesus laid down his life so that we could know forgiveness in a life-changing way. His call for us to live out that forgiveness became a priority for him. He said, "If you forgive other people when they sin against you, your heavenly Father will also forgive you. But if you do not forgive others their sins, your Father will not forgive your sins."

"The righteous will thrive." Honestly admitting when you are wrong, apologizing, and forgiving lead to healthy living. Splinter removal is the defining mark of those who are serious not just about surviving life but also about thriving. It is your mark. It is your signature. It is your soul tattoo. It is called forgiveness. It is how you, with God's help, remove the splinters.


## A CARPENTER'S SECOND CAREER

Betrayal. Lies. Abandonment. Neglect. Abuse. _____. You name it. The list is long and bleak. The list sends little splinters flying everywhere. Little forests have cropped up between you and others. What are you to do with a forest? Find someone with a mighty chainsaw?

Jesus spent most of his life working with wood. Maybe that's why he understood the beam/splinter metaphor on several levels. He grew up around wood. Carpentry was the family business. His dad taught him how to handle the tools and how to shape the wood. He smelled of sawdust and had wood chips in his hair. He knew a thing or two about removing splinters.

For Jesus, wood was something to be shaped. He measured it, sawed it, scraped it, chopped it, sanded it, pounded it, and transformed it. He took raw material and fashioned it into something useful and beautiful.

Have you ever seen a carpenter's hands? They are strong and capable, with a lot of calluses. After decades of patiently fashioning wood, Jesus turned to the work of transforming lives. He extended mercy to help people thrive. Jesus grew up in carpentry but entered the public eye as a healer, teacher, rabbi, and miracle man.

On one occasion there was standing room only as Jesus had packed a small home in Capernaum. People were elbow to elbow to get a better look at this man whom everyone wanted to meet. As the crowds leaned in to listen to his words, four men carrying a fifth man, their friend who could not walk, made their way toward the house. When it seemed impossible to get through the crowds, one of the four men, holding a corner of the mat, considered their options and pointed to the roof. They all nodded in silent agreement. Reaching the top of the steps and setting down their friend, they tore back the roof covering until they had a man-sized hole.

As the brazen men lowered their friend through the hole smack-dab before Jesus, the crowd stirred, wondering what he would do. Jesus looked first at the man lying before him, then up at the hole in the roof, and finally at the four waving down from above. Jesus smiled. Here the splintered wood and need for healing came together. What did Jesus do? He declared the paralyzed man's sins forgiven. His buddies on the rooftop were startled; that was not why they had come. They broke through the roof for a different reason. They had heard Jesus could heal people.

Some religious leaders reacted to the same words. Forgiveness of sins? Only God had the authority to pardon transgressions. Why would Jesus exonerate this man from his offenses before God? Jesus knew exactly what they were thinking. Staring straight at them, he asked them if it was easier to forgive sins or make a paralyzed man walk. Jesus left them tongue-tied, knowing neither was easy nor humanly possible. He then turned his attention to the paralyzed man, extending his hand. Without hesitation, the man grabbed Jesus' carpenter-turned-physician's hand, stood up, and walked in front of that huge crowd.

Everyone was astounded by this miracle worker who could forgive something that only God could forgive and heal as only God could heal. Jesus was like no one they had ever known. It is an incredible thing to be forgiven. Washed clean. Set free. A clean slate. A new beginning. A fresh start. A splinter removed.

Jesus, God in the flesh, that carpenter miracle worker, forgave the sins of those who looked to him in faith, and when he extended that mercy,

> forgiveness
> detached
> the
> soul
> splinters.

That man walked away from the house in Capernaum a new man. Not only could he walk, but his soul was set free. He had been released from the weight of guilt from every lie he had ever told, every offense he had ever committed, every thought and deed that had been displeasing to God. What a sight to behold! A man who could walk again. What a sight to behold! A man who walked in freedom.

Jesus was an expert in splinter removal. He talked about forgiveness, he extended forgiveness, and he lived out forgiveness. Jesus was so passionate about forgiveness that he died for it. His life was defined by it. This carpenter who spent his life working with wood would believe in forgiveness so much, he would die on a piece of wood talking about forgiveness as he breathed his last: "Father, forgive them, for they do not know what they are doing." These were some of the last words that came from the mouth of Jesus.

We cannot experience the forgiveness of Jesus without having our entire beings changed. The paralyzed man experienced a dramatic shift both in his spirit and his body. The gospel story shows the power of God able to completely change everything about an individual, both body and soul.

The gospel story describes, first, a need to recognize our unrighteousness—our unrightness in relationship to God and others. Unrighteous lives are filled with broken relationships. The good news is that Jesus came to this earth so that all our relationships could be made right, be restored. There is beauty in recognizing our brokenness because we then get to experience radical forgiveness from God through Jesus. God removes our soul splinters.

That same forgiveness still changes people. It changed me.

I was faced with a choice as a young woman to either extend forgiveness to someone who betrayed me or let bitterness haunt my life. A solid friendship of eleven years came to a screeching halt when that friend started seeing my boyfriend behind my back. I was out for blood. But a patient and persistent pastor reminded me that Jesus' forgiveness changed everything and allowed me to eventually forgive. My life had been changed because of Jesus, and his challenge was now for me to forgive as Jesus had forgiven me. It took some time, but that forgiveness and freedom finally came.

Being forgiven by the expert in forgiveness is an amazing experience. It extends clear through your very being. It is absolute.

Sometimes we have to experience forgiveness, feel forgiven, and see it happen to us to truly understand what forgiveness means. Only then can we sincerely forgive others because we know how incredible it is for someone to release us from pain that we have inflicted.

## BUT CAN I FORGIVE MYSELF?

Sometimes forgiving ourselves can be the hardest of all in this restoration process. Trusting that God could forgive us, even for the things we do not talk about, is hard to believe.

When you do not *feel* as though you deserve forgiveness, sometimes the best thing to do is let your *head* talk to your *heart*. When our feelings do not match up with what our heads are telling us is true, we have to keep saying it until it sinks into our hearts. The Bible says that when we confess our sin before God, God throws our sin as far as the east is from the west and remembers it no more. God loves the world and reconciles people relationally. The Apostle Paul wrote,

> If anyone is in Christ, the new creation has come: The old has gone, the new is here! All this is from God, who reconciled us to himself through Christ and gave us the ministry of reconciliation. . . . Be reconciled to God. God made him who had no sin to be sin for us, so that in him we might become the righteousness of God.

Through Jesus, God was ready to reconcile the planet, generation after generation. Splinter after splinter. I am not a math expert, but that is a big number with a whole lot of zeros. God wants to see a whole lot of lives thrive. Your choice is a precious gift that was given to you to be exercised with responsibility and care. To reconcile. To remove the splinter.

## RECONCILED RELATIONSHIPS

We are to forgive others for the ways they have wronged us. Sometimes doing this is exhausting and difficult. When a disciple asked Jesus if he should forgive someone up to seven times, Jesus responded by multiplying that number by seventy. Jesus invites us to forgive often so that we can be forgiven often.

Jesus wants us to be a people who can forgive one another; a carpenter skill he wants to pass on to all of us is how to remove splinters. First he extended this forgiveness to us so we could experience it. Then he said, "OK, now it's your turn."

With Jesus as a model, we know a life that thrives practices forgiveness. Even when it is hard. Even when we do not want to do it. This isn't a sugarcoated throwaway comment such as, "It's OK . . . whatever." That's putting a Band-Aid on the splinter without taking it out. I'm talking about acknowledging brokenness and seeking restoration in that relationship, or at least in that situation, to the best of our ability.

To thrive, we reach into the places of hurt in our lives and extend forgiveness. To thrive, we let go of the pain, anger, hurt, and rage we have for a person or institution and what he, she, or it did. We cannot always mend the relationship. And I am pretty sure that we cannot ever completely forget. It's said that Clara Barton, founder of the American Red Cross, was once reminded of an egregious wrong done to her years earlier. She acted as if she didn't know what the speaker was talking about. "Don't you remember it?" she was asked. "No. I distinctly remember forgetting it." Barton understood that we cannot let the wound become so infected that it becomes toxic. When we let that poison remain inside us, it changes us. It changes our mind-set. It changes our relationships. It changes our right relationships. We don't want to trust others. We don't want to risk getting hurt again.

*Failure to thrive* (FTT) is a medical term given to a child whose physical growth over time is way below the norm. In adult medicine, FTT describes someone who is not doing well physically, possibly for dietary reasons or poor self-care. FTT describes a condition more than a specific disease. Thriving is a condition—something that can be changed. That means you can make changes that will lead to a life that does not just survive but thrives.

Forgiveness is the process of letting go of the pain and the poison that the situation has caused to fester within you. And the first step in this process is valuing introspection. We talked about this in the first chapter. You acknowledge that you've been hurt and you've felt wronged. Something happened. In time, it might be clear that you misunderstood motives or that you somehow contributed to the situation, but for starters, it's helpful to admit that something is wrong in a relationship, something has happened, you're in pain, and you need relief. Denying the problem (denying the pain or infection of the splinter) isn't helpful.

Recognize the consequences for your life that have resulted because of someone's hurtful words or actions. Admit how you wish things would have gone. Forgiveness does not condone the actions of others. It does not excuse inappropriate behavior. Forgiveness is not a stamp of approval. Wrong actions and offensive words are still wrong.

Jesus calls us to forgive even when it is hard and even when we are not at fault. Once the splinters are removed (no matter how painful), the wound can begin to heal. You likely will never be the same. The wounds can be deep. Forgiving people for something they did to you gives them back those little pieces of wood that have been lodged in your heart. Actually, you do not even need to hand them back. Just drop them or throw them. Fling them out of your life. Let the healing begin.

Sometimes the splinter is lodged too deep. Sometimes removing the splinter involves asking Jesus to enter the situation with tweezers to dig and pull that splinter out of you. Sometimes it involves tears. Sometimes removing the splinter causes you to bleed, and sometimes a cartoon Band-Aid doesn't help much.

Remember all the time and energy that you spent thinking about it and hurting because of it? Forgiveness says, "I am not going to let this affect my life anymore. I am not going to be consumed by anger and hate any longer. I am forgiving you by releasing the impact of your actions on me." Mercy removes the splinter. Forgiveness plucks it out and drops it on the ground. Go ahead and step on it for good measure.

Go ahead and have your *Braveheart* moment . . . "FREE-DOM!"

Then tell the person, if you can and if it is safe to do so, that you have forgiven him or her. This is not for that person's sake. The offender might not even realize he or she wounded you or how deeply the wound affected your life. But verbalizing the reality of your forgiveness is an important solidifying step. You can gain important closure of the situation by verbalizing forgiveness.

Sometimes it is just impossible to make a broken relationship right. Extending forgiveness is one thing, but that forgiveness may or may not be rightly received. You can be responsible only for your part. If the other person involved refuses to meet you halfway, you have to make your peace, knowing that you tried. If the other person is dangerous or toxic, do not put yourself in that place of danger. That is not freedom. Sometimes you can love people best from a distance.

It doesn't mean you love them less. It means that you love them and yourself by not letting them hurt you again. Right relationship means that you discover the appropriate way to relate to others. Sometimes it means spending more time with a person; sometimes it means spending less or no time with a person. If the offending person is no longer in the picture and you cannot find peace, you may want to speak the forgiveness to God or to a trusted friend.

Forgiveness can take time. Some things can be forgiven quickly, and other things take a lifetime to work through. Often wounds have built up over years; sometimes scabs have formed over the splinters, and inflammation or scar tissue lingers. But God understands complicated relationships. When you commit to the process, God honors your intent and helps you extend forgiveness—even if incrementally. God loves to see forgiveness, which is an amazing, beautiful, mind-blowing, mystifying thing.

Forgiveness is a miracle, a gift from God, who pulls out the splinters in your life. It takes time, effort, and practice to bring that forgiveness to others. Commit to the process. Invest in it. Make a decision to be a person of forgiveness. Pull out those splinters. Change your world. Change your family tree. Change your life. Thrive.

## DISCUSSION QUESTIONS

1. When have you had to remove splinters?
2. When have you been forgiven for something?
3. How do you struggle to forgive others?
4. Is there a particular person you are struggling to forgive?
5. Do you know someone who forgives well?
6. Are you committed to thriving in life enough to make efforts to reconcile broken relationships?
7. How will you begin to take steps to forgive?

*Obstacles are those frightful things you see when you take*
*your eyes off your goal.*
*—Henry Ford*

## CHAPTER 5

# LIVE OUT LOUD

## *The Celebration of a Worthy Pursuit*

T HE FIVE-AND-A-HALF-MILE Rose Parade has to be one of the greatest parades. This annual spectacle began in 1890 in Pasadena, California. It ushers in the New Year, a prelude to the Rose Bowl football game. The city starts setting up months in advance. The sidewalks seem to expand to include bleachers and Porta-Potties to accommodate an estimated 700,000 people who pour into the city. Groups camp out on New Year's Eve, complete with sleeping bags, hibachi grills, and lawn chairs to claim front row seats along the blue-line route perimeter. The New Year is celebrated all night long. Silly string and party poppers rain down randomly. Noise makers and boisterous people electrify the atmosphere.

Mine is among thousands of families trying to maintain an annual tradition of driving into Pasadena on New Year's morning. A minor pre-parade celebration happens in our car when we find a free parking spot, even if we have to walk six to eight blocks to reach the parade route. The city parking vendors make out like bandits, with cars filling every possible nook and cranny. On the parade route we see extended ladders and overturned buckets—anything that a person can sit or balance on to get a view over the heads of the crowd. My kids find the best seat in the house is often perched on Dad's shoulders. With anticipation we strain our necks to catch the first glimpse of the parade. Then suddenly an awe-inspiring black stealth bomber flies overhead, signaling the start of the Rose Parade.

And the parade begins. Every Rose Parade float is covered with real flowers and seeds; only living organic matter is allowed. The drifting aromas waft along the air currents. We ooh and aah over each float, trying to determine which one is our favorite. Roses and intricately arranged flowers are turned into just about anything you can imagine: eyeballs, racetracks, waterfalls . . . Flowers are not just things of beauty; they become a designer's paintbrush.

And the music. Marching bands from all over the world assemble to compete and blast out tunes of celebration. The crowds clap, sing, and cheer them on.

I'll never forget the wide-eyed wonder of my two-year-old. He clapped with and for the music. From our lawn chairs lined up in the second row right near the blue perimeter line, he cheered on the floats and pointed to the balloons. When a chair opened up in front of us, on the very front row, with permission he plopped himself down just in time to welcome a new marching band. This marching band suddenly broke formation and clumped in groups to serenade the sidelined spectators. It was really cool, very creative, loud, and completely traumatizing for a two-year-old. He jumped back to my arms, clinging, crying, and yelling, "Marching band scare me!" He repeated that mantra for months. Most kids get scared of the monster under the bed; mine was scared of marching bands, though he has outgrown the fear and learned to love a loud parade.

Parades live out loud: immediate, vibrant, colorful, noisy, and breathtaking. Living out loud means moving as a parade moves, marching forward with singular purpose toward a worthy goal.

What is your live-out-loud purpose in life? What pursuit is worth your full focus? It is a big question. Overwhelming even. When you do not know what to do with your life, go back to what you *do* know: God loves you and wants you to thrive. To thrive, you must be committed to righteousness, that is, right relationship with God and those you live with and encounter. This book focuses on one of Solomon's proverbs: "The righteous will thrive." Another proverb of

Solomon reads, "Commit to the LORD whatever you do, / and he will establish your plans." You will fulfill your *teleios*, your purpose.

Just as it takes incredible planning and preparations to put together a memorable parade, it takes intentionality to put together a memorable life. A life that thrives lives out loud by setting goals. Setting goals allows you to be intentional with your purpose and make the most of your time.

## STRIVING FOR A GOAL

Clear goals that are set and implemented, step by measured step, can lead to success because goals give you something to strive for. They give you a sense of purpose. They keep you growing as a human being. "The plans of the diligent lead to profit," as another proverb relates. Goals can take an ordinary day and make it extraordinary. Goals can provide a sense of accomplishment and achievement to help you feel productive, help you contribute to your neighborhood, to society.

Goal setting might even seem overwhelming because if you set a goal, you have a target for which you are aiming. What if you miss? What if you do not make your goal? The fear of failure can be enough to prevent the best of us from setting a goal. But what if you don't fail? What if you meet that goal? Don't look now, but you are thriving.

Goals do not have to be big. You do not need to end homelessness, famine, or global warming and create world peace by next Tuesday. Maybe, though, you could give a homeless person a hygiene kit and a lunch by next Tuesday. Maybe you could clean out the garage and have a yard sale. Maybe you could file that stack of paperwork or set up the family's dentist appointments for the year. Maybe you could drive a little less or carpool. Maybe you could have your neighbors over for pizza or help create a neighborhood garden.

When I begin to set goals, I aim for two to three goals per month, then print them out and place them on my desk at home and in my day planner. That way I can stare at them and remember that I want to accomplish these specific things in a given month. For example, in January my husband and I sit down together and plan our budget for the year. We figure out what we are going to spend each week and each month. Each dollar gets a name. Some goals are repeated each year. In February I start working on our vacation plans for the summer. In March I do the taxes and set up medical physicals for the family. In April I plant the spring garden and set up dentist appointments. In May I have a yard sale and schedule a family photo shoot. In June I do meal planning and devotions planning for the year. In July I plan for family's and friends' birthdays and anniversaries. In August I set professional goals and plant the fall garden. In September I work on our family holiday schedules and a family photo album. In November I work on an annual fitness plan. In December I prep for Christmas.

There are always way more things that I want to do than what I can get done. But if I don't put something on the calendar, it will not get done. My goal planning is fluid. I can add, delete, and move things around if they fit better in a particular month for some reason, but at least these priorities are in front of my eyes regularly.

Goals are a way to be specific about our ideals and allow us to practice what we believe. Goals give us direction and chart a course to guide our behaviors and actions in a way that allows us to accomplish our heart's ambitions. Goals help us keep time, money, and relationships in line with our purposes. It is so easy to procrastinate or get sidetracked. Goals make sure that we do some things that we always say we would like to do. We are to "press on toward the goal to win the prize." By making right relationships our target, we can align our goals with them.

## IF WISHING MADE IT SO

Some things we cannot change. I wish I was taller. Yes, I can wear killer heels, but at the end of the day, I'm still only five feet two inches. Other things we could change, but instead we use wish language as a way to grumble our way through a situation. I've taken three languages in my time at school, and with each one, the experience has been miserable for me. I am not good at languages. I usually find myself wishing I was good at languages or wishing I'd gotten a better grade. The reality is that if I had studied more or practiced more, I probably could have gotten a better grade.

Wishing can make you feel better about complaining. Watch out, though, because goals will bring change. If you wish your family was different, you do not have to do anything but sit back and criticize Aunt Matilda and whine about your stepbrother, Joe. However, if you set a goal to make the relationships within your family better, you are now involved in the process of change. You are committed to being part of the solution. You are invested.

Making a wish is much easier and involves less work than setting a goal and trying to achieve it. We wish upon falling stars, watching in wonder, as they twinkle through the sky. We wish upon them because it is a magical moment.

Falling stars are rare to see, especially in or near a city. And because they seem to disappear as soon as we see them, they're a difficult sight to share with companions. We wish upon a star because it is an unexpected and rare spectacle that we feel privileged to see. Perhaps in that special moment, we have the attention of the divine, so we close our eyes and make a wish hoping that magic stardust lands on those thoughts and makes them come true.

People have been watching stars, making wishes, and associating them with divine powers for a very long time.

You may think of the star that led the wise men to baby Jesus in Bethlehem. Or how about the Big Dipper? The legend is that the Greek god Zeus put his lover, a nymph-turned-bear named Callisto, into the sky for safekeeping. The Big Dipper is formed by the brightest stars of this Great Bear. There is something significant about these sparkling jewels in the night sky that cause us to reflect on the divine. Perhaps they are our link to the heavens.

Some use stars as a catalyst for prayers offered up to the heavens. Disney has locked the idea into our hearts and minds with the song "When You Wish upon a Star." Wishing is magical. Wishing is the stuff of songs and fairy tales. Achieving goals, however, takes work. Wishes involve chance; goals involve change.

Every year you have a birthday. Sometimes it is a great excuse to have a party, bring out the cake loaded with candles, and make a wish. The tradition of candles on cakes can be traced to the ancient Greek and also German traditions. There is a long history of people believing that the smoke takes wishes up to heaven.

A wish combines the reality of a yearning with a magical rare moment. We want that special moment—that particular exceptional experience—to be the thing that brings change. We all want change to happen effortlessly. But change happens intentionally. To achieve our goals, we need to pursue them.

## WHERE THE TIME GOES

Have you ever set a goal and worked to achieve it? The process requires more than spouting a New Year's resolution; it involves creating a plan. An end goal can be relatively easy to set. By March I want to . . . But achieving that goal will require that you shape your days with intentionality and use your time differently than you currently do. I took piano lessons as a kid. I was terrible at it. Doing things that you are not good at makes time go . . . by . . . so . . . slowly. To heighten my misery, I had a metronome and felt ticktocked to death. That little thing moved back and forth keeping a perfect rhythm. It sat next to me pounding out an exact beat, demanding that my time must conform to it.

As much as it was an excruciating experience for me, that metronome helped meld my notes into a rhythmic harmony. That little tool helped time become my friend so that I could make music. That's what we need as we set out to achieve a goal: a way to harness our time to see that goal come to fruition.

Time. We all have it. We all waste it. Often we wish we had more. To achieve our goals, we must be intentional about how we use it. What do we say yes to? What do we say no to? Where do you waste precious time? On your phone, in front of the TV, on the computer? It is amazing how all the little things we do throughout the day add up.

Make friends with time. Move into action: grab a pen or bust out your computer. Get ready to set goals that help you thrive. I've included a few goal exercises to get the juices flowing.

First up is a time exercise. Figure out where time goes so that you can befriend it to accomplish your goals. Fill in the Time Table with how you spend each hour in your day (not how you *wish* it was spent). Start by filling in the largest blocks of time first, such as sleep, meals, work, or school.

## TIME TABLE

| | Sunday | Monday | Tuesday | Wednesday | Thursday | Friday | Saturday |
|---|---|---|---|---|---|---|---|
| 5:00 a.m. | | | | | | | |
| 6:00 a.m. | | | | | | | |
| 7:00 a.m. | | | | | | | |
| 8:00 a.m. | | | | | | | |
| 9:00 a.m. | | | | | | | |
| 10:00 a.m. | | | | | | | |
| 11:00 a.m. | | | | | | | |
| 12:00 p.m. | | | | | | | |
| 1:00 p.m. | | | | | | | |
| 2:00 p.m. | | | | | | | |
| 3:00 p.m. | | | | | | | |
| 4:00 p.m. | | | | | | | |
| 5:00 p.m. | | | | | | | |
| 6:00 p.m. | | | | | | | |
| 7:00 p.m. | | | | | | | |
| 8:00 p.m. | | | | | | | |
| 9:00 p.m. | | | | | | | |
| 10:00 p.m. | | | | | | | |
| 11:00 p.m. | | | | | | | |
| 12:00 a.m. | | | | | | | |
| 1:00 a.m. | | | | | | | |
| 2:00 a.m. | | | | | | | |
| 3:00 a.m. | | | | | | | |
| 4:00 a.m. | | | | | | | |

Filled in? So what did you discover? Is time your friend or your enemy right now? Don't feel guilty. It is impossible to use every hour wisely. The goal is not necessarily efficiency all the time but focus and well-used time. Even God took one day off to rest and enjoy the newly created world. Sometimes we need to live spontaneously in the moment and see what God brings across our paths.

But here we're focusing on using time to achieve goals. Now, think and pray over your time usage. How should you spend it wisely, redemptively, purposefully? Grab a high-lighter and mark schedule blocks where you would like to see change. In what hours of the day and week would you like to use your time differently?

## A BIOGRAPHICAL SKETCH

Now that you know how you spend your time, let's look at what you actually want to do with your time from this moment on. Let's think through what it would mean for you to thrive. How would you describe your life if you were thriving? Jot down a short goal biography. *Here's my description of my hoped-for life, abundant life—fulfilling the purpose for which God created me. My life is awesome. Here's why . . .*

As you write, remember you want to do more than wish this was true. Add in things that are important to be realized.

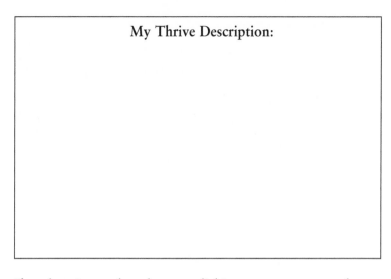

**My Thrive Description:**

If goal setting and goal accomplishing are new to you, do not panic. Setting and accomplishing goals is a bit like putting a puzzle together. The goal is the completed puzzle. The goal-setting process and the goal-accomplishing process take each puzzle piece, one at a time, and find where it fits. Pretty soon, you have put the puzzle together and accomplished the goal.

## SETTING REALISTIC GOALS

Based on what you would like your life to look like, as described in My Thrive Description, try to create specific goals toward that end. Consider the following pointers:

*Take a pass on setting one* big *life goal.* Having a single major goal can be completely overwhelming and inhibit you from taking the steps you need. Plus, you are an ever-growing, ever-changing human being. Your goals need to grow and change with you. Your goal should not be to attain your Thrive Description. That is too big a goal. Think in terms of specific aspects of the big picture that you can manageably change.

*Understand that down-to-earth goals rock!* Write down something that is possible for you to accomplish in a set time period. What could you accomplish by next Tuesday that is out of your ordinary routine? How about a month from Tuesday or a year from Tuesday? What could you plan or organize? What could you change or create? What could you add or delete from your schedule?

*Choose bite-sized portions, please.* When in doubt, think of something you'd like to see happen as taking bites of a meal. Each of the things on your plate hopefully gives you a well-balanced meal, but you cannot eat them all at once. You choose which bite to eat when. A goal can be one food group or even one bite of that meal. Set yourself up for success, not failure. It is much more rewarding and motivational if you can start to check some things off the list.

*Establish a timetable.* Once you have decided what you would like to accomplish with your goals, you need to establish a timetable in which to complete them. What pieces can they be broken down into to create the process? Give yourself enough time to work on the goal so that you can complete it with excellence. Write down a tangible date that gives you a time boundary in which to realize this goal.

*Reward yourself.* Having a built-in reward can help you

keep your eyes on the prize. Just make sure your reward is appropriate. If your goal is to lose weight, your prize should not be chocolate cake! My college roommate always got a motivational reward from her mom that she dangled like the proverbial carrot from her desk; it was her prize for finishing finals each semester. Heed the words of Philippians 3:14: "I press on toward the goal to win the prize for which God has called me heavenward in Christ Jesus." Your reward can also be a great place to keep things relational. Celebrate your accomplished goal with friends or family.

*Don't work your goals alone.* Accountability partners can be a great motivational force for you. Training partners are invaluable when you have set a physical goal. An encouragement team is healthy. This is a wonderful way to keep your goals rooted in relationships as well. Let others be part of your life. Let them cheer you on.

## Goal Examples

| Goal | Goal Date | Process | Reward |
|------|-----------|---------|--------|
| Sign up at the local soup kitchen | Next Friday | Research local soup kitchens (Monday) Call the two that are local and seeking help (Wednesday) Go to chosen soup kitchen to go over scheduling (Friday) Evaluate first free day to serve at soup kitchen (next Wednesday) Schedule monthly commitment and | Coffee house in the city I like to visit, after my time in the soup kitchen |

| Goal | Goal Date | Process | Reward |
|------|-----------|---------|--------|
|  |  | confirm with soup kitchen by next Friday (with one trial run in place) |  |
| Establish a budget | Next month | Establish my budget categories (this week) Collect my bills from the last year (next week) Total my bills and divide by 12 months (next week) Assess our total income (third week) Assign each dollar a name in the budget (fourth week) | Movie night at home with popcorn |
| Run a marathon | Next year | Determine what marathon and date Establish training schedule Get appropriate training shoes and gear Find training partner/ team Train | Marathon picture on Facebook |

What are five Thrive Goals you could set to begin to accomplish your Thrive Description?

| **Thrive Goals** |
|---|
| 1. |
| 2. |
| 3. |

```
┌─────────────────────────────────────────────────┐
│  4.                                             │
│                                                 │
│  5.                                             │
│                                                 │
│                                                 │
└─────────────────────────────────────────────────┘
```

Now let's set a plan to achieve some of these goals. Circle the three areas that you would like to work on first. For three goals, write down at least three steps for your goal process and a time frame that will lead you toward your reward. Action steps might include scheduling a particular time in your day to work on this goal, finding a friend to hold you accountable in this area, reading a book or enrolling in classes on the topic, devoting some (how much?) money to this goal, praying (when? for how long?) for wisdom in this area, and so on.

Goal Process

```
┌─────────────────────────────────────────────────┐
│  Thrive Goal 1: Action Steps                    │
│  1.                                             │
│  2.                                             │
│  3.                                             │
│                                                 │
└─────────────────────────────────────────────────┘
```

```
┌─────────────────────────────────────────────────┐
│  Thrive Goal 2: Action Steps                    │
│  1.                                             │
│  2.                                             │
│  3.                                             │
│                                                 │
└─────────────────────────────────────────────────┘
```

Thrive Goal 3: Action Steps
1.
2.
3.

As you wrote down these goals and action steps, you were establishing life priorities. You have focus. You have clarity. You have a mission. Watch out. You are thriving.

## MAKING FRIENDS WITH TIME

Let's go back to the original chart (last time, I promise). Now that you have established goals and priorities with purpose, make plans to re-establish your schedule. How can you work with the time God has given you to meet these goals? Goals are created out of what you value. Your heart beats for these priorities. God loves to see you living out your purpose. Passion with focus is unstoppable. You will thrive.

Fill in the chart again. This time indicate how you think you could best use each hour. Again, fill in the largest blocks of time first, such as sleep, meals, work, or school. Then look at the time you have remaining to accomplish your goals. Keep in mind that this is only a weekly schedule. You may want to create a chart that works better for you. Personally, I use this chart. It is a great way for me to examine my priorities and goals whenever life feels too busy, too full, or too unbalanced.

|  | Sunday | Monday | Tuesday | Wednesday | Thursday | Friday | Saturday |
|---|---|---|---|---|---|---|---|
| 5:00 a.m. | | | | | | | |
| 6:00 a.m. | | | | | | | |
| 7:00 a.m. | | | | | | | |
| 8:00 a.m. | | | | | | | |
| 9:00 a.m. | | | | | | | |
| 10:00 a.m. | | | | | | | |
| 11:00 a.m. | | | | | | | |
| 12:00 p.m. | | | | | | | |
| 1:00 p.m. | | | | | | | |
| 2:00 p.m. | | | | | | | |
| 3:00 p.m. | | | | | | | |
| 4:00 p.m. | | | | | | | |
| 5:00 p.m. | | | | | | | |
| 6:00 p.m. | | | | | | | |
| 7:00 p.m. | | | | | | | |
| 8:00 p.m. | | | | | | | |
| 9:00 p.m. | | | | | | | |
| 10:00 p.m. | | | | | | | |
| 11:00 p.m. | | | | | | | |
| 12:00 a.m. | | | | | | | |
| 1:00 a.m. | | | | | | | |
| 2:00 a.m. | | | | | | | |
| 3:00 a.m. | | | | | | | |
| 4:00 a.m. | | | | | | | |

OK, so put it into practice. Keep your chart in a place where you can see it. Refer to it often to see how you are doing. What adjustments do you need to make? What made sense on paper but is now unrealistic in practice? Make notes and alterations as you go to prepare for tomorrow or next week. Remember this is more of a guideline, not a requirement. It is meant to be a helpful tool, not one that stresses you out or makes you feel guilty.

You are allowed to change your goals anytime. Make them smaller and more realistic or make them bigger and more audacious. You have this one life to live, and no one is going to live it for you. Do not get to a place where you look back and regret the decisions that you made or the way you spent your time. It will take some sacrifice and hard work to get where you want to be, but imagine what it will be like to be there—thriving.

## BRING OUT THE BAND

This chapter is titled "Live Out Loud" because achieving your goals is a good reason to party! These accomplishments are cause to throw a parade-sized party when you are living in a way that achieves your purpose. Regardless of your temperament, living out loud is not about being loud. It is about thriving. Whether you prefer to celebrate boldly with lots of people or have a little party on the inside with just you and God, you can thrive.

## DISCUSSION QUESTIONS

1. What is something you have wished would happen in your life?
2. Have you ever made it a goal?
3. What do you need to do to increase your focus on this goal?
4. How can you invest your time to see this goal happen?
5. Who could be a resource to you in seeing this goal to fruition?
6. What is your time frame for realizing this goal?
7. Who could hold you accountable about this goal?
8. How do you think this goal will help you thrive?
9. Who does this goal impact?
10. What did you learn from your making-friends-with-time exercise?

*I have told you these things, so that in me you may have peace.*
*In this world you will have trouble.*
*But take heart! I have overcome the world.*
—*Jesus*

CHAPTER 6

─────────
─────────

# DRAGON SLAYING

*The Freedom of Vanquished Fear*

I FOUND A BABY LIZARD in my house. The tiny thing was hiding in our dining room. Little monsters like this (and big ones) live in the sewers, under the bed, and in the closet. Unfortunately, our world seems so full of monsters that our first response is fear. From a very young age we experience fear—fear of being left alone, fear of the dark, and fear of those green vegetables that appear on our plates at dinnertime.

Thankfully, the monster under the bed is not real. Neither is the one in the closet or the sewer, for that matter.

We have the ability to become afraid of almost anything. Ablutophobia is the fear of taking a bath. Consecotaleophobia is the fear of chopsticks. I have a friend who is afraid of flowers. (Yes, it has a name: anthophobia.) What prompts fears that may seem irrational? If you were attacked by a dog as a child, maybe you have a dog phobia (cynophobia). If you were taught to be afraid of people who are different from you (xenophobia), then you likely experience that fear. It may be irrational and unfounded, but when you are taught something, it becomes part of who you are until you question it, unlearn it, and replace it.

As children, we seek comfort by leaving the light on or sleeping with our parents to avoid being alone. As adults, we do not have the luxury of something that so easily calms our fears. Fear is a powerful force that often motivates illogical behavior. We lose a little bit of rationality when we are staring a monster in the eyes.

Some fear is healthy. It can even protect you. When I first moved to California, I anticipated spending time at the ocean. Some of my new friends took me to the beach and showed me how to bodyboard along the waves. I jumped on that board and completely nose-dived it into a huge oncoming wave. I crashed and went under the water. While the waves pounded over me, my life flashed in front of my eyes. Thankfully, one of my friends reached down and grabbed me out of the water. I might have fared better if I'd had a healthier fear of the waves.

As humans, we have a natural built-in self-preservation mechanism. We are hardwired to survive, and fear in the face of a traumatic situation can kick our senses into overdrive. Anything we perceive as a threat to our survival causes an imbalance in our equilibrium. Our physical bodies gear up for one of two responses: fight or flight.

The fight-preservation mode can enable you to accomplish feats beyond your normal capacity. Faced with a traumatic situation, people are able to lift cars and downed trees that they would not normally be able to lift.

The flight-panic mode can also protect you, let's say if you are a pedestrian running from an oncoming car. Proverbs 22:3 says, "The prudent see danger and take refuge, / but the simple keep going and pay the penalty."

I wonder if there's a third option, evidenced by ostriches. Many believe that ostriches bury their heads in the sand to avoid danger. But that's not what they're doing. These big birds that can't fly actually just fall forward in the sand and collapse their heads to the ground so that they will look like bushes to a passing predator. The mama ostriches are especially good at doing this to protect their eggs. These poor birds get a bad rap for being foolish in the face of danger when, in reality, they are pretty smart. They take action and outsmart the fire-breathing dragon. Clever.

The ostrich cannot escape danger but can be wise in the face of it. An ostrich must have courage to survive its predators. And so must we. We must be wise and have courage to thrive despite real threats from those who try to steal our joy, rob our hope, push us down, and dare us to survive them.

Forty million Americans suffer from an anxiety disorder—that is, they are coping with or living with some form of fear. Maybe you are one of them. We all have moments of stress and anxiety, but when our lives are controlled by a fear, we have stopped living with purpose and freedom. We cannot thrive when we live in a constant state of fear. Right relationships are not defined by fear.

## WALLOWING IN WORRY

There's so much to worry about. Just read or listen to the daily news. Corruption. Perversion. Exploitation. Unfortunately, there is a very real dark side of the human race. Humanity is both brilliant and baneful. Those who live only for selfish gratification wreak havoc on our planet. Fear infiltrates our hearts because of their ability to prey upon our apprehensions.

Parents wonder what kind of world their children will grow up in. The challenges that our children will face are complicated, extensive, and downright overwhelming. It is enough to put fear in hearts everywhere. These fears are not easily dismissed with a nightlight. And yet our vague worry gets us nowhere. Jesus told his listeners, and us, that today, this day, will bring "enough trouble of its own." Worrying about the future only brings unnecessary anxiety.

How can we thrive amid such stress? The Apostle Paul encouraged us to fight fear by redirecting our thoughts to focus on "whatever is true, whatever is noble, whatever is right, whatever is pure, whatever is lovely, whatever is admirable—if anything is excellent or praiseworthy—think about such things."

## THINK ON THESE THINGS

"Behold the turtle. It only makes progress when it sticks its neck out," said James Bryant Conant (1893–1978), a chemist and president of Harvard University. Like a turtle, we can make progress, but it takes sticking out our necks a bit. Take time to identify what is causing the fear in your life. Name your monster. It could be a low-grade anxiety that slowly pushes your feet into wet cement. Or it could be something that is creating full-blown panic attacks. Regardless, half the battle is to understand your enemy and assess if he or she truly is a threat. Is there clear and imminent danger? Or are you creating a scenario that does not truly exist for you?

Sometimes if we can determine the root of the fear, we can find some freedom from its tyranny. It takes time and work. But the reward is freedom from the fear. *Freedom.* Doesn't that sound good?

As we try to get to the bottom of your fear, a good place to start is to ask yourself questions, the hard ones that are easier to avoid. When did the fear start? When do you experience that fear? Is there a certain time of year or time of day? Is there someone who seems to trigger it? Have you ever had a time when you did not experience it? What was the difference in that situation and when you did experience it?

Working through some of these questions with God by your side, with a friend, or with a professional can bring clarity and healing. You might even get to slay that dragon.

As you seek to extricate that fear from your life, you can replace it with truths that will feed your soul. Find the truth. Seek the truth. Live in the truth. There is great power in the truth. The truth can drive fear away: "You will know the truth, and the truth will set you free." Do you love the truth? Do you crave the truth in your life? Do you need the truth to thrive? Yes. The truth leads to freedom.

How easy it is for the truth to get a bit bent and corrupted until it becomes an untruth. Nine out of ten people will not walk under a ladder because they believe that it will bring them bad luck. Is this true? Lies work so well because they play upon our fears and at some level have an attractive quality. Having a relationship with God is a good way to seek out the truth because the core of God's very being is pure and integrity filled. The Bible offers a solution to fear through a relationship with God. A verse written by the prophet Isaiah assures those who have a friendship with God that one major step to overcoming fear is embracing that relationship:

> So do not fear, for I am with you;
>> do not be dismayed, for I am your God.
> I will strengthen you and help you;
>> I will uphold you with my righteous right hand.

## FIGHTING FEAR

"Courage is doing what you're afraid to do. There can be no courage unless you're scared." So said Eddie Rickenbacker, an American fighter pilot and number-one American ace during World War I, who received the Medal of Honor for his service. He knew something about being in terrifying, life-threatening situations.

What are some steps that you can take to develop courage and fight fear? If you find yourself paralyzed by fear, especially if you are taken by surprise, a physical response to a threat may be so severe that you start to hyperventilate; that is, you breathe too quickly and feel faint. If this happens, intentionally slow down your breathing and breathe through pursed lips, as if you were whistling, or through your nose. Try to breathe so that your stomach, more than your chest, rises and falls. When you are in a panic, try to regain your physical equilibrium, keep your bearings, and maintain your wits, confident that "the righteous are as bold as a lion."

Another way to develop courage? Take every thought captive so that you control your thoughts rather than letting them control you. Here are some ways to do that:

*Create flash cards* that have scriptures on them about living with courage and fighting fear. Every time you are faced with a fearful situation, pull them out and say them aloud. Commit some to memory, and they will be there waiting for you anytime you need them. Consider these examples:

I can do all [things] through him who gives me strength. (Philippians 4:13)

Even though I walk
   through the darkest valley,
I will fear no evil,
   for you are with me;
your rod and your staff,
   they comfort me. (Psalm 23:4)

I am the LORD your God
   who takes hold of your right hand
and says to you, Do not fear;
   I will help you. (Isaiah 41:13)

Be strong and courageous. Do not be afraid or terrified because of them, for the LORD your God goes with you; he will never leave you nor forsake you. (Deuteronomy 31:6)

So we say with confidence,
   "The Lord is my helper; I will not be afraid." (Hebrews 13:6)

*Write those words on your life.* Have on hand a few dry-erase markers. Write the scriptures above (or others) on the mirror so that when you are getting ready in the morning you actively engage with them and see yourself through their power. Say them out loud, making a verbal pronouncement that today you will fight your fear.

*Turn to God.* From the first book of the Bible to the last, righteous men and women have turned to God for strength in the face of fear. The Apostle Paul mentioned the power of the name of Jesus:

> God exalted him [Jesus] to the highest place
> and gave him the name that is above every name,
> *that at the **name** of Jesus* every knee should bow,
> in heaven and on earth and under the earth,
> and every tongue acknowledge that Jesus Christ is Lord,
> to the glory of God the Father.

When fear, either real or imagined, begins to infiltrate your being, try repeating Jesus' name—not in a flippant, irreverent way but rather as an act of faith, a prayer for stabilizing peace. Proverbs 18:10 assures us that "the name of the LORD is a fortified tower; / the righteous run to it and are safe."

*Have a means of encouragement.* A good old-fashioned pep talk can also give you the encouragement you need to move beyond the fear. Maybe you need to look in the mirror and give that pep talk to yourself. Write one in advance so that you have the words ready to go in front of you.

Perhaps you have a friend or a family member who would be willing to be this encouraging advocate for you. When you have people who believe in you, you start to believe in yourself. If they think you can do it, maybe you really can. When you are in right relationships with people, you can lean into those relationships for support. Relationships that have been nourished and provide a balance of back-and-forth care are strong enough to survive.

If you are only beginning to develop these righteous relationships and do not have trusted friends, ask yourself another question: Where can I go to meet people who would be willing to invest in me, pray for me, and encourage me? Make plans to go to and spend time in a soul-refreshing place. Church might be a good place to start, or a support group. Take a courageous step, and put yourself in good situations with good people to create good relationships.

*Name the fear.* Write down your fears when they start to set in. Sometimes it helps to get them out of you and transferred to paper. When you look at them in black and white, they might give you a whole new perspective. Write them down in a journal, and then evaluate them through a series of questions:

- When did this fear set in today?
- What was I doing when it started?
- When was the last time I had this fear?
- Is this a real fear, or have I imagined it?
- Write down some of the scriptures noted above. How can they specifically help overcome this fear?

- Pray through these fears, and then go back and write down any perceived answers. Did you find this to be a great encouragement? Could you see how God has helped you deal with them? If God has helped you in the past, God's faithfulness is a good sign that help is available for this current fear.

*Use your prayerful imagination.* When a fear comes, sit down and prayerfully imagine taking this fear and placing it in a box. Pick up the box, and carry it to Jesus. Give it to him. Leave it there with him. Remind yourself of Jesus' promise: "Come to me, all you who are weary and burdened, and I will give you rest."

Trust is the opposite of fear. We trust in things all the time. We trust other drivers to stay in their lanes. We trust that restaurant food is safe. We trust the fire department will come to the rescue if we have a fire. It is important to trust in the *right* things, however. Trusting in the lottery to pay our bills probably won't work out well. Because of God's faithfulness, we don't need to live in fear. We can live in the security of knowing that we can trust God. God shows faithfulness by keeping the promises that were made in Scripture. Jesus was a fulfillment of God's faithfulness. Having a relationship with Jesus means that you never have to face fear alone.

I once read a story about a young man carrying great anxiety about his marriage and went to consult with his pastor. The pastor listened and then asked if he'd prayed about his distress. "I've prayed about it day and night for over a week," the husband replied. Toward the end of their session the pastor prayed and then urged, even coached, the young man to pray aloud. "I can't," he responded. With insight the pastor suggested that he hadn't been praying but rather worrying "day and night." To help the young man turn worry to prayer, they turned to a psalm, which helped the man verbalize his fear and appropriate heartfelt trust.

## STEPPING OUT WITH COURAGE

As our thirty-second president, Franklin Delano Roosevelt inherited an overwhelming job as the world was in an economic depression, and Americans were tired, downtrodden, and afraid of the future.

FDR was the perfect president for that particular season because he had already dealt with large fear issues in his own personal life. As a young man, he was healthy, muscular, and athletic. Then at age thirty-nine, he contracted polio in the summer of 1921. Facing the fear of losing mobility, FDR fought to regain the use of his legs, particularly through swimming. He was eventually able to walk with crutches but spent most of the rest of his life using a wheelchair, winning the election as governor of New York in 1928 and president in 1932, when nearly every bank in the nation was closed and unemployment was pervasive. In FDR's first inaugural address on March 4, 1933, his famous words rang clear: "Let me assert my firm belief that the only thing we have to fear is fear itself." He courageously led the country toward recovery, his New Deal program creating national parks, new roads, and new hope for Americans.

When Roosevelt faced the winds and fears of World War II, he crafted the four "essential human freedoms," claiming that these must be accepted worldwide: freedom of speech, freedom of worship, freedom from want, and freedom from *fear*.

Wisdom and courage go hand in hand as a dynamic duo to face down the fire-breathing dragons that threaten your well-being. Not only do you need the moxie to step toward the dragon, but you also need to have a plan to escape getting scorched. Dragon slaying requires bravery, accurate assessment, and fast footing. You have to keep moving. When you let fear paralyze you, you become dragon food.

I think also of the courage of Rosa Parks, who's been called "the first lady of civil rights" because of her refusal to give up her bus seat to a white passenger. Parks's 1955 stand, which prompted the Montgomery bus boycott, became an important symbol in the civil rights movement. Even though she is viewed today as a courageous hero, at the time she was arrested for her resistance, and she lost her job as a department store seamstress. But fear did not paralyze her. When she moved to Detroit, she continued her fight against racism. She found the courage to look past her personal fears for the good of others. Rosa said, "I have learned over the years that when one's mind is made up, this diminishes fear; knowing what must be done does away with fear."

You were created for courageous living. How do you live courageously? How do you become more courageous? Begin with small steps. Building boldness can require a courageous leap. But small steps work too. Once you step out for small things, your courage muscles are better able to endure bigger challenges.

I don't like spiders. I used to be able to get away with asking other people to get rid of them. But now I am a parent to little people who are really scared of spiders. I am their protector. This whole shift in mind-set has changed my attitude and my behavior toward spiders. I am bigger and faster than those ugly creepers. I still dislike them, but I now leap out of my chair in a single bound to face down the spider crawling toward one of my toddlers. I do not hesitate. I move with swiftness and sureness.

Do something today a little out of your comfort zone that will help to build your courage. Once you conquer that one thing, it is not so scary the next time. And if you did it once, you can do it again. Even if you did it badly, you still did it. And it is bound to be better the next time. If it is not, then dig your feet in, get determined, and persevere. You can beat it. Go back and break it down again and find a smaller step to give yourself a victory. Even small victories can build your confidence, which leads to courage.

## A NEW KIND OF FEAR

You were not created to hide in fear. You were created to know peace, a deep soul-satisfying peace—God's peace. The Hebrew word for "peace" is *shalom*. *Shalom* is not just the peace of no conflict. It is a more holistic peace that includes restoring relationships. *Shalom* is a common Jewish greeting, and early Christians greeted one another with "grace and peace."

Peace leads to a life that thrives. It leads to a kind of satisfaction and enjoyment of life that are incomparable. A heart at peace has little opportunity to know fear.

Fear may highlight the news, but it does not have to dominate your life. Give peace a chance. Let peace reign in your soul. Can you imagine life where fear is held in check by something more powerful? A life that is focused with purpose and fears conquered—that lives a *shalom* peace of God? Rise up with courage. You can do it. Go slay a dragon.

## DISCUSSION QUESTIONS

1. Who do you admire as a courageous person?
2. When has fear been a distraction in your life?
3. Name the fire-breathing dragons in your life at the moment.
4. How would your life be different without these fears?
5. What is your plan to face them?
6. How do you develop courage to confront them?
7. How does a right relationship with God give you courage?

*The only thing necessary for the triumph of evil is for good men [and women] to do nothing.*
—Edmund Burke

C H A P T E R   7

# SWAT

## The Honor of Fighting Injustice

I HAD A FLY OUTBREAK in my house. No joke, I think they hatched in my house. I swatted down more than twenty-three flies in a couple of hours. I could not find where they were coming from. The invasion of the flies coincided tragically with having a shrieking two-year-old who was completely horrified by the buzzing little devils. No one messes with my baby, especially not a bug-eyed flying insect. Now I am pretty dang good with a fly swatter. Bring on the chopsticks.

We have bigger issues than flies, however. Swarms, hovering just out of reach. They create distractions. They bite.

We meet the swarm daily: the buzz of the dark side of humanity, the shadow side.

These malicious insects do not play for team humanity; they play only for themselves. They buzz, sting, and bite. And they contain a dark side that pays homage only to self-gratification. They completely overlook the suffering and pain inflicted upon others for the sake of personal profit and pleasure. They chomp on other humans. They sting their hope.

Just recently the nation was shocked by the news of twenty children and six adults shot in a public elementary school in Newtown, Connecticut. The gunman, Adam Lanza, entered the school and randomly shot children, teachers, and staff. This reckless disregard for life is so shocking, so horrible, it is hard to comprehend. The sting of injustices spans the globe, from poverty in the African Sudan to poor communities in the inner cities of the United States. But even in the midst of endless stinging wrongs both locally and internationally, there are individuals who stand up and fight to right the wrongs that victimize the poor and defenseless.

Murder. Rape. Drugs. Alcohol. Pornography. Prostitution. Fraud. Domestic violence. Child abuse. Kidnapping. Slavery. Robbery. Environmental exploitation. Greed. Profiteering. Identity theft. Terrorism. War. The "flies" seem to multiply and invade places and people at alarming rates. A whole swarm of attitudes and behaviors needs to be challenged and changed.

As a person striving for righteousness, a person striving for right relationships with God and others, you have an opportunity to overflow beyond yourself, to wash out destructive attitudes and behaviors. Want to thrive? George Washington Carver offered these words of wisdom: "How far you go in life depends on your being tender with the young, compassionate with the aged, sympathetic with the striving, and tolerant of the weak and the strong. Because someday in life you will have been all of these."

A life that thrives involves fighting for righteousness— right relationships with God and others. "The righteous will thrive." This is the essence of justice. The ideas of righteousness and justice are so closely aligned in the New Testament that the Greek word *dikaiosynē* can be translated as either "righteousness" or "justice." Justice is the side of God that seeks to right the wrongs that we create.

God's answer to the world's injustice was to forge a new humanity, a new community, a new body. To bring life out of death. God's answer began on Sunday morning and continues to today. The truth is, God is always acting for justice and righteousness, and God has invited us to participate in that action. God asks us to stand up for those who are not able to do so. He wants us to be the voice for those who are voiceless. But how can we be the voice for the voiceless? Power for the powerless?

When my oldest son discovered that batteries made his toys more fun, he was always looking for them. If a toy wasn't fun enough or seemed to stop working, he immediately asked for batteries. For him, batteries were his go-to solution. Every human has an empty power pack, ready to be filled with God-sized batteries. No more cheap, generic knockoffs that only run for a few minutes. Only use the best. Part of having a right relationship with God is having God's presence with us and empowering us. God's power is able to fill us to go beyond ourselves. God can give us more energy, more passion, and more power to accomplish what God calls us to do.

## FIGHTING WELL

There has to be something that makes you really mad when you hear about it or see it happen. God has planted deep within you a sense of justice because God is just. And you are created in the image of God. God has always had a heart for those who are taken advantage of. Rabbi Nancy Fuchs-Kreimer notes that the "widows and orphans frequently represent all economically vulnerable people, especially in passages in Deuteronomy that set up a crude system of redistributive justice for a primarily agrarian society. . . . These rules are reflected in the story of Ruth, saved from starvation by gleaning in the fields of Boaz." Widows, orphans, and foreigners in the land. God has not forgotten these people. Neither should we.

So what gets your blood boiling? What makes you mad? Righteous anger is not anger that belittles or lashes out to make you feel better by hurting someone else. It's not anger that buzzes or makes you part of the swarm. Righteous anger goes back to our root meaning of *righteousness*: right relationships with others and with God. Righteous anger causes you to get riled up because you are involved in something or see something relationally that is not right. Either a relationship among people or a relationship with God is not right. A wrong needs to be righted.

You cannot escape it; you are involved. You may never darken the doors of a seedy, dark, and unrighteous place, but you are still involved because you are part of the seven billion human beings on this planet. You are involved because part of your team is down.

An estimated twenty-seven million people alive today are trafficked into slavery. Internationally and domestically, slave traders and owners kidnap, buy, or sell people—mostly women and children—for sex and/or labor, as if people were a commodity for profit. The enslaved people have had one of their God-given rights as human beings taken away: their choice. Freedom. They have no say in what they do today or tonight or tomorrow. If they do not obey what someone else wants them to do, they will be tortured or abandoned or killed.

It is as if a big infestation of evil is sweeping over our planet. How do we punch holes in this kind of prevalent darkness?

According to the Bible, Jesus fed five thousand people in one sitting. That was one big dinner party. The thing is, Jesus had no food for them. Five thousand hungry people packed around him, looking at him for help. That was an overwhelming situation. Jesus told his leadership team, the disciples, to feed the people. They came back to him saying there wasn't anything they could do. There weren't enough resources. No food. No money. Not enough help. They couldn't do it.

Jesus asked them one question: What *do* you have? They had two fish and five loaves of bread. And five thousand people. No way was it enough. They could not even make a dent.

Jesus said, "Give me what you have." And Jesus did the miraculous. He took responsibility for feeding the people. He asked the disciples only for their obedience and the offering of what they had. And that is what he asks of us. When we seek justice in overcoming the huge giants of injustice, we humbly offer our five loaves of bread and two fish. When we bring what we have to Jesus, give it all to him, and trust him, Jesus is able to move in ways beyond what we could ever imagine.

Jesus came with power for the powerless. I love that. I love that someone with power wants to help those who do not have any. Very few people use their power for good. Most swarm to get power. But the Bible tells us:

> He has shown you, O mortal, what is good.
> And what does the LORD require of you?
> To act justly and to love mercy
> and to walk humbly with your God.

Showing goodness does not have to be all the way around the globe. You can act justly and love mercy right where you are. That is using power for good to punch holes in the darkness. Even when it seems like such a small hole, a light makes all the difference.

I'm sure Joybelle thought she had no power when she, as a young Christian, reluctantly accepted the challenge of her pastor's wife, Jo Anne Lyon, to silently pray what Frank Laubach called "flash prayers" for strangers or passersby on the street. Traveling to work by bus in the predictable company of complaining commuters, she agreed to pray for these fellow travelers for one week. Jo Anne tells the story:

> When we met the next week, Joybelle reported that not much had happened, but sending flash prayers had at least kept her mind off of the complaint-filled conversation that surrounded her each morning. I encouraged her to try the experiment for another week. . . .
>
> The next week Joybelle noted that people on the bus were not complaining so much, and people seemed to engage in conversation more. That was not a dramatic start, but Joybelle kept praying. Eventually, she was able to start a daily bus Bible study for commuters which lasted for several years. . . . In that daily bus ride, she discovered the blessing of purpose.

You have a particular mix of gifts that no one else has to impact your world. No one else has your combination of personality, natural gifts, education, past experiences, and resources. Do something with those gifts. One step gets you pointed in the right direction. And sometimes it involves collaboration. Would Joybelle have started a prayer ministry if she hadn't been encouraged by Jo Anne? Prayer is essential. Ask questions. Do research. Have conversations. Write a check. Volunteer.

Can you imagine if we had seven billion human beings with all their genius thriving on this planet? What would it look like? It's mind-blowing, isn't it? How do you bring your gifts to the table? Here are basic, important starting points:

*Purchase wisely.* If you use your money in a way that brings justice, you are making a huge statement. Look for fair-trade labels. Look for clothing that is made in slave-free environments. Fair-trade and sweat-free mean those products have been made without slave labor. It means people are getting paid reasonable local prices for their work. If you can't purchase everything wisely, offset your purchases with donations to organizations that can establish and empower fair trade and sweat-free markets and commerce. Supporting your local farmers and farmers' market can save on fuel consumption, invest in a local economy (that is, neighbors), and provide healthier food for you.

*Prevent ignorance.* Educate yourself and others about world affairs, including regional abuses, needs, and worthy causes. Read. Watch documentaries. Investigate. Learn about a different country—or a local neighborhood—every week.

Once you have information and a sense of what you can give, it is hard to sit complacently.

*Promote legislation* that provides consequences for those who abuse and exploit human beings. Prosecute those who stir up the dark side. Pay attention to the laws forming in your state or local jurisdiction. Sign petitions to strengthen laws to protect the weak and vulnerable. "Do not exploit the poor because they are poor / and do not crush the needy in court." It is up to us to create a community, a world that protects and treasures life. I think of William Wilberforce, a member of Parliament who spearheaded legislation to outlaw the slave trade in England. He and Christian friends—men and women of some influence and means—"ended up expending themselves—day-in and day-out, year-in and year-out—seeking more just public policies for people far removed from themselves and their social class. They thereby left us a powerful model of what the Christian pursuit of justice and the common good is all about."

*Participate in a group* that encourages social justice. Teamwork is a wonderful way to combat injustice. As you pool your resources, you can likely influence more lives. It is also essential to have the support of others when fighting darkness. It is so easy to get discouraged and overwhelmed. Working alongside others allows you to cheer on one another through difficult moments.

Check out local churches, colleges, or community centers. If you can't find a group, start one. It takes just a few like-minded people passionate about doing good to make a difference. Gregg A. Ten Elshof points out an exemplary aspect of a "healthy group": it has "a realistic sense of its own limitations and vulnerability. Its existence is not threatened when its members disagree. And, while it may be united by a common cause, its members have a sensible view of the relative worth of that cause as compared with other goods."

*Provide resources.* Part of participating is contributing resources and donating time. Our church provides backpacks for local girls and women who are rescued off the street from a life of prostitution. These freedom bags contain a hygiene kit, yoga pants, T-shirt, underwear, socks, flip-flops, water, a snack, a journal, a Bible, a blanket, often a small stuffed animal, and a handwritten note extending love. These bags arrive in our office packed full of goodies, but they are really filled with hope. We partner with local law enforcement to provide these bags to the rescued girls and women. One girl immediately removed her high heels and heaved them into the garbage as she gratefully reached for the flip-flops that came with no obligation. One FBI agent noted that it was the highlight of his career to give that freedom bag to a minor. Another girl, with tears running down her face, said it was the first thing anyone had ever given her with nothing expected in return.

*Form relationships.* Forming a relationship with someone who has been victimized can be a wonderful way to help bring restoration and healing. Specialized training is often necessary and usually helpful in understanding the process of healing for particular issues of trauma. At our church we have opportunities to work with women and children who have been victims of domestic abuse. This is a great way to offer love to people who have felt very unloved. Preventive relationship building can be even more powerful. Mentoring, tutoring, and employing youth and at-risk adults can thwart darkness from getting a foothold in lives. Sharing a bit of your own experiences can encourage others along the way. Everyone needs people to cheer them on in life. You can be the voice that makes the difference for someone else. We also have a few teams that have relationships with youth shelters. One team goes and bakes with the girls there once a month. Sure, the cupcakes are delicious, but the ministry of presence is invaluable.

*Pray.* Ask for God's guidance to know how you can impact our world. Join in the work that God is doing in your neighborhood or across the globe. Maybe you want to connect with International Justice Mission (IJM). IJM is on the front lines rescuing people, often families with young children, from lives of slavery. Brick kilns, factories, cocoa plantations, farms, fisheries, and brothels enslave innocents for profit. IJM and other amazing organizations fight relentlessly to kick down those doors and bring freedom and hope.

Grab your fly swatter and kill some swarming flies. *Swat!*

## DISCUSSION QUESTIONS

1. Where do you see injustice in the world?
2. What makes you mad when you see it?
3. Are you more inclined to learn about injustice or hide from it?
4. Who do you know that is fighting for justice?
5. When have you fought for something worthwhile?
6. Where do you see complacency in your life?
7. What things come easily to you?
8. How do you think you could use these areas to promote justice?
9. Are you on team humanity?
10. How do you plan to join the fight for justice?

*Dum spiro, spero (While I breathe, I hope).*
—*Latin proverb*

CHAPTER 8

─────────

# RANDOM RAINBOWS

*The Triumph of Hope*

S HEETS OF RAIN SLAM INTO your windshield. You hold the steering wheel in a death grip. Your heart thumps. You are not entirely sure if the tires are still gripping; you seem to be gliding along the road. It is pouring rain, the cats and dogs kind. Where did this storm come from? How could the sky hold so much water? Then all of a sudden, it stops. The skies clear up. The dark clouds roll away.

Then, out of nowhere, the sky is lit up with a spectacular array of colors. Minutes ago your life flashed before your eyes, but you now realize that you will survive. You might even thrive.

Unfortunately, we get way more storms than rainbows. When a huge rainbow appears in the sky, people start clicking photos. The natural phenomenon is the artwork of God. It seems to echo Emily Dickinson, exclaiming, "I dwell in Possibility." After an unparalleled storm, God put the first rainbow in the sky to serve as a promise. The colorful sky stamp was to remind survivors—and their children from all generations till now—that they could move forward in life. They could start anew. They could thrive on this planet.

## WHAT MAKES YOU STRONG?

Righteous living is hard. It takes a whole lot of patience to put up with (and love and thrive alongside) people. It takes a kind of strength that most of us are not born with. We can have the best intentions for being people of righteousness, having right relationships, and none of us will get it right all the time. We are not that strong or kind all the time, every day, in every situation.

What makes you strong? If you walk around the gym, you will see all kinds of people pushing themselves to gain strength. Gaining physical strength takes training and repetition, perspiration and dedication. It takes discipline. Strength training helps you feel confident and competent to face a situation. So how do you get emotional and spiritual strength to face life? How do you find strength for your soul to go on?

There is an often overlooked strategy and building block for soul strength that can help you thrive: *hope*. Real hope is often stealthy and not as easy to find as its cheap imitations. Just as a rainbow sneaks into the sky, hope can sneak up on your soul and change everything. Hope can light up your soul and give you rare strength. It can also come after heavy rains. Precious. Amazing.

## HOPE IS NOT . . .

Hollywood makes great movies about dreams coming true. Musicians write inspiring songs about wishes and dreams. They fill us with anticipation of what might lie ahead. My daughter had a princess party when she was four. She ran around the house with a magic wand yelling "poof," wanting things to fly. Wishes are fun, but *hope* is real.

And hope is not just positive thinking. Positive thinking is more of a corrective or systematic procedure used in psychology for reversing negative thinking or pessimism. Positive thinking says that you can will yourself out of a situation by thinking about it differently. Positive thinking puts the responsibility for change on you and your ability to reason your way through life. Positive thinking says you must learn to see the glass as half full rather than half empty. But having hope is different than putting a spin on how you view things.

When I was in college, I had a summer job at a resort on a beautiful lake in northern Michigan. Families and groups often stayed for a week. As a waitress, I got to know the families while I served them gourmet meals throughout the week. Occasionally, they invited me and other employees to go out on the water with them in the afternoons or evenings. I was excited to finish up the season with the final days of water-skiing. It was a perfect evening; the lake was like a mirror. I was first up on the skis. The skis were a little big, but I thought they'd be fine. The boat had some problems, though, and sputtered out on my first two attempts to get up. The third time I was up and skimming across the water.

Everything was beautiful until I tried to jump the wake. One ski fell off, and the tip hit the water and flipped me over, slamming my back on the calm, clear water that was like cement. My legs went numb. For a few moments I envisioned being paralyzed. Slowly, though, the feeling came back into my legs, but my back was injured. It was easy to let hopelessness set in as my mobility was greatly challenged in the days and weeks that followed. The doctor prohibited me from driving for a while. Standing in my friend's wedding became difficult. Beginning a new job on campus became problematic. My body did not work the same way it had before the injury. Those days it was easy to feel defeated and hopeless. Every day became about wishing I could do the things that I could not do, and I was spiraling down into hopelessness.

The journey to regaining strength in my back challenged me to learn to hold on to hope when plans are interrupted, even if it means life looks different from what I envisioned.

Hope has a quality of something beyond ourselves and our goals. It says that something outside us can affect this situation. Hope can do something that we cannot do. Having hope means trusting that this universe holds more than the power of people. It is a belief that God holds it all together.

Real hope is ultimately rooted in the one who created all things, the one who created you and me. Hope is this wonderful, powerful, and easily overlooked perspective that is extended to us with an open hand. Hope can be seen in Michelangelo's painting on the Sistine Chapel ceiling of God's hand reaching out to Adam's hand. Hope lies between those hands.

The God of hope has not lost connection with humanity but rather continues to extend a hand, so as to "fill you with all joy and peace as you trust in him, so that you may overflow with hope by the power of the Holy Spirit."

Hope, which is all about the future, hasn't always been a valued characteristic. The ancient Greeks, being fatalists, discounted hope. Euripides even called it "man's curse." But the biblical writers understood its critical importance to their physical survival and spiritual well-being. Jeremiah recorded: "'I know the plans I have for you,' declares the LORD, 'plans to prosper you and not to harm you, plans to give you hope and a future.'" Hope is one of the major themes of the Bible, beginning with the story of creation. God, in his goodness, wanted to redeem his good but marred creation.

The thrive master of the Bible, Jesus of Nazareth, said, "I have come that they [you and I] may have life, and have it to the full [thrive]." A full life—not a life packed with activities and commitments, but full and abundant. Rich. Not the money kind, but the satisfying kind. It is a life rich with the blessings of the human experience.

Hope's high point was the resurrection of Jesus. Arthur Gordon wrote that "the Easter story of the Resurrection is the most stunning proclamation of hope ever heard on this planet." The Resurrection is God's promise that things do not need to stay the same. Things can and will change because of Jesus.

How can one person meet each of us in that place where we feel alone? That place where we feel misunderstood. That place where we feel unvalued. Jesus is able to reach into the soul of each individual on this planet who seeks him and ignite hope in each one's heart. His promise is that anyone who seeks him will find him. Anyone. Anywhere. Anytime. This one person, Jesus, had the righteousness that Solomon talked about down so completely that he could become the living, breathing hope for you and me. This hope is the secret to a life that thrives.

## LIVING FOR SOMETHING BEYOND OURSELVES

The last time I was in the Middle East, Starbucks had made it to Israel but not many of the surrounding countries. Since some of the surrounding countries did not have the real thing, they improvised and formed coffee shops called Stars and Bucks and other variations. Their efforts were creative, but unfortunately, their creativity did not compare favorably with the real thing.

Jesus spent three years of ministry extending hope and freeing people from their past so that they could live in real hope. Not Stars or Bucks, but the real thing. On one occasion Jesus was teaching a large crowd gathered around him in a public square, the Temple courts of Jerusalem. Out of his peripheral vision he saw a woman being dragged by some of the religious leaders. Jesus finished his sentence as he carefully watched her being pushed with harsh hands as she stumbled forward. She covered her face with her hands, grasping her head covering tightly, but the tears were still evident in her eyes. The religious leaders accused her of adultery and demanded her punishment according to the law.

Jesus looked first at her and then at her accusers. He directed their attention to the ground. He was still sitting there, as he had been while he was teaching. He smoothed the ground in front of him and began to write in the sand. The accusers could not be patient, they could not wait, and they wanted action. As the questions poured over Jesus, he straightened and said to them, "Let any one of you who is without sin be the first to throw a stone at her." He continued to write in the sand.

The accusers left, but the woman remained standing there. Jesus spoke directly and publicly to this shamed woman. He spoke words that extended hope. Jesus became her hope. I do not condemn you. You are forgiven. Start over. Do not make the same mistake. Learn from it. Live. Thrive.

"Everything that was written in the past was written to teach us, so that through the endurance taught in the Scriptures and the encouragement they provide we might have hope," wrote the Apostle Paul, who pointed us to this wise book to find hope. There is a promise that if we fill our lives with the things of God, we will become more hopeful. Hope is so essential to our existence that abounding in hope is one thing that should define us as human beings.

In the Bible the Apostle Paul famously grouped hope with two other virtues—faith and love. Perhaps when hope is hard to find, we need to join these three forces. All three push us to live beyond ourselves and call us to something that we are not currently able to experience with our own resources.

Here are two classic ways of looking at the three foundational virtues: "Faith goes up the stairs that love has made and looks out of the windows which hope has opened," and "Hope rests on faith, love on hope, and victory on love." As you can see, they are intertwined. Let's look at them in the order that the Apostle Paul mentioned them: faith, hope, and love.

## FAITH

Faith asks for confidence in someone other than ourselves. Faith leaps when we are not positive what is on the other side. Faith risks so that our hope can land somewhere. This is not a call to blind faith. We learn to develop healthy trust based on past experiences. We believe in those things that have been successful. We doubt or abandon those things that have failed. The Bible does not call us to check our minds at the door or to have blind faith. Instead, our faith seeks understanding. Our faith trusts because we've tested it, and God has proved worthy of our trust.

## HOPE

Hope is an intangible that you cannot touch with your hands, yet when it boldly enters the scene, it reshapes everything. Hope is the presence of optimistic expectation. Hope is the boost of endurance to carry on. Hope is the glimmer of joy in the midst of sorrow. Hope removes the splinters.

Hope is the promise of something yet to come, calling us to anticipation outside what we are currently experiencing—

something that is better than the present. Hope is going to bed on Christmas Eve, anticipating Christmas morning.

Hope is the promise of new life. Hope anticipates the good just around the corner. It smells expectation. Our ultimate hope involves knowing that there is more to this life than what we presently see and experience.

## LOVE

Love requires relationship, which means that love requires us to go beyond ourselves. Like hope, love anticipates the good. Love calls us to selflessness. Love puts someone else's needs and well-being above our own. Love compels us to do things that we would not normally do, to go the extra mile. Love connects us so that hope can move among us. American clergyman and abolitionist Henry Ward Beecher observed, "God puts the excess of hope in one man in order that it may be a medicine to the man who is despondent."

In the chapter titled "Hope" in her book *Why Jesus Makes Me Nervous*, Joy Jordan-Lake tells of her venture as a young woman moving to Louisville for grad school but foolishly without having made any housing arrangements. Seeing her predicament, friends of a friend—a couple with two young children—took her in until she found a place of her own:

When I left their house, they sent me off with gifts—both big hugs and also my first pieces of furniture: a bed . . . and a Bentwood rocker. . . .

Just last weekend, the old wooden bed they gave me two decades ago as I began a hopeful new season of life was passed on to a family just leaving a homeless shelter for a hopeful new season of their own. Hope: sometimes passed on in word, and sometimes in the form of slats and a sturdy headboard.

These three intangibles—faith, hope, and love—combine and help us live beyond ourselves. They give us cause and momentum to thrive.

## HOLDING ON TO HOPE

I love anchors. I love to take the boat out on a warm, sunny summer day and anchor it on a sandbar. The waves gently lap against the boat, but the anchor holds it steady. We picnic, we play in the water, and we jump off the boat into the refreshing lake. Hope is like that anchor. It can be a gentle reminder that we are held in place by the hand of God. Hope is vital for us to claim and hold: "We who have fled to take hold of the hope set before us may be greatly encouraged. We have this hope as an anchor for the soul, firm and secure."

Imperative. Important. Essential. We have to be so famil-iar with hope that we know how it works. Hope does not get used up. You do not have a hope allowance that sets off an alarm when you have hit your limit. Hope has an amazing capacity to expand and spread. Hope regenerates. It springs up in unlikely places, in multicolor splendor, a rainbow.

Holding on to hope means that on days when bad news comes, maybe again and again, you may have to fight harder. You may need people who are hopeful to speak into your life. Proverbs 13:12 states, "Hope deferred makes the heart sick, / but a longing fulfilled is a tree of life." Letting go of hope can make you emotionally unhealthy. However, when hope is realized and fed, it brings health into your soul. When you feel as though hope is thin, envision how God could work through the situation. Envision how God's glory could be revealed to you and others through this time. This is hope.

When my heart was broken in a relationship that I was hopeful could end in marriage, I had little hope for my future. I quit eating, sleeping, and hoping. Yet I kept fighting for hope. Some days by shedding a lot of tears and some days by crawling. Slowly putting the pieces of life back together is making a statement of hope. Sometimes getting through the basics of life—eating, sleeping, exercising—is all we can do. Meeting the basics of survival can be making a statement of hope. Taking care of yourself on this basic level means you are choosing life. You are choosing to survive one more day. You are making a statement of hope that tomorrow may be better.

People need hope to survive the complicated lives we lead. Even the people of the Bible needed this call to hope, this call to continue to live, to choose life as a declaration of hope. Moses urged the people of Israel, "This day I call the heavens and the earth as witnesses against you that I have set before you life and death, blessings and curses. Now choose life, so that you and your children may live and that you may love the LORD your God, listen to his voice, and hold fast to him. For the LORD is your life."

Although the biblical book of Job can be hard to read, it can be helpful to us. Job had everything taken away from him—his health, his family, and his possessions. But the book doesn't end there; it takes us through Job's emotional and painful process of loss and hopelessness and back to restoration. As Job worked his way through this traumatic season of life, wrestled with God, and clung to hope, God blessed Job with abundance. Author and professor Leslie Williams writes,

> When we are stuck in a situation that feels hopeless, useless, and miserable, it is good to do a quick review and see how God has pulled together seemingly random strands of our lives in the past to accomplish His purposes. Somehow knowing that He has always been with us (and is currently with us even if we don't feel His presence) gives us the courage to continue with the Kingdom task at hand—especially when the task seems impossible.

## HANGING UP HOPE

I have four metal letters that spell *H-O-P-E* hanging on a wall in my house. Honestly, it was a bit of a process to get them. A friend in Michigan had them, and once I saw the set, I went in pursuit of those four letters. Those letters and my friend inspired me. But when I was visiting Michigan and went to the store, all I could find was *H-O-P*. I was optimistic, hopeful, that I could get that last letter to complete my word. My best friend persistently tracked down the *E* for me and sent it across the country to California so that I could change my *H-O-P* to *H-O-P-E*.

We've moved around a bit and have hung the letters in many of our rental homes through the years, or I should say my husband has hung them for me. Each letter has to be measured out, leveled, and aligned with the others. *H-O-P-E* takes work.

When we finally bought our home, I was ready to hang up *H-O-P-E* for good. I was so excited, but we couldn't agree on where to put it or how far to space the letters apart. Finally, we compromised. *H-O-P-E* took some intentionality. I happily get to stare at my giant *H-O-P-E* every day. It's a reminder that we need to hold on to hope but also that we have had *H-O-P-E* spring up in the most amazing places in our lives.

Hold on to hope. Cling to it. Maybe even hang some hope in your house. Give hope the last word. Let hope be the champion. Let hope prove itself strong.

# DISCUSSION QUESTIONS

1. When was the last time you saw a random rainbow in the sky?
2. Who do you consider strong among the people you know?
3. Where does their strength come from?
4. Do you consider yourself strong? Why?
5. When have you been surprised by hope?
6. What do you think about this understanding of hope as strength?
7. Do you believe that living with hope can make a difference in your life?
8. How do you think you can practice being a person of hope?

*Adopt the pace of Nature. Her secret is patience.*
*—Ralph Waldo Emerson*

CHAPTER 9

DON'T WASTE
OXYGEN

*The Peace of a Reasonable Pace*

A S A KID I CONSIDERED myself part fish. The underwater world was just so much fun. The sand squished beneath my toes and became a conforming seat if I could get all the way to the bottom. The minnows gave fish kisses as they nibbled on my toes. Shells were mini-treasures hidden in the sand while seaweed gracefully waved its bright green arms.

The garbled sounds of the world above the water hovered about my ears. Everything slowed down underwater. Tiny bubbles escaped my nose as I slowly leaked air out. I loved those contests to see who could stay under water the longest. I knew my swim teacher was timing our group as the waves gently lapped around us. I was aware of my fellow classmates who were one by one popping to the surface and filling their lungs with fresh, clean air. I stayed underwater. I knew I could win. I had practiced. I had discovered that if I took a few big breaths before I went under the water, I could hold my breath longer. And then, hunkered down, I held really still.

When my swim teacher tapped my shoulder, signaling for me to come out of the water, I realized I had won. I was excited for my victory but a little annoyed that she made me come up before I needed to. Even though my lungs were starting to get tight and I felt the pressure of needing another breath, I could have lasted a few more seconds.

Breathing is one of those things that you take for granted until you go underwater and, unless you truly are part fish, cannot. Breathe in. Breathe out. We do it thousands of times a day. The average person takes about fifteen breaths per minute. If we multiply that by sixty minutes in an hour and by twenty-four hours in a day, we get 21,600 breaths per day. Give or take a few breaths, based on whether you've been making it to the gym or eating a lot of potato chips.

Ironically, something that is absolutely essential for our existence is invisible. We cannot see the darn stuff that we need to survive. We trust it is there, and we expect there to be enough for us every day. Seven billion people on this planet depend on oxygen for survival, and there is enough. We do not seem to be able to distribute enough food and water for everyone on our planet, but we have enough air. We do not need to hoard it or save it.

Unless you are underwater—and then there is not enough oxygen for you. That tank of air or those big breaths will take you only so far. You have to pace yourself when you are underwater. The faster you move, the more energy you expend, and the more oxygen is required. Move fast and use up your oxygen, or move slowly and make it last.

Every day we make decisions about how to pace ourselves. Is it a triple-espresso kind of day or a lie-on-the-couch-and-veg kind of day? We drift in and out of the seasons of life. Some are busy; some are slow; some feel insane. To thrive in life, we need to understand pace.

## PACE IS PERSONAL

Comedians like Jay Leno and David Letterman are masters at pace. A joke doesn't work without perfect timing. People pay attention to them because they have genius pace.

Pace is important in running. Sprinters know how to make a burst of energy count. Long-distance runners who run too fast at the beginning of the race burn out before the finish. Those who have pace-trained know how fast they can run to maintain their speed and energy. They are prepared to go to the distance. They are equipped for success. They may even win the race. Pace matters.

Pace is not the same for everyone. Your pace and mine could be completely different, and both of us could still thrive. My thinking is clearer and my writing improves when I am fresh in the morning. But because I do everything better in the morning, I try to do everything in the morning. Not a good idea. There is not enough time in the morning to get it all done. Since opposites attract, and God has a sense of humor, I married someone who is a night owl. The key is to find the pace that works for the life God has given you.

Near my home is a hill that beckons me to pick up a bit of downward speed. When my kids are with me, my two-year-old often calls from his car seat, "Slow down, Mommy, slow down." Ironically, when he is running at breakneck speed so that I can barely catch him, he doesn't notice his speed. But when he is strapped to his car seat in a moment of rest, he notices mine.

The responsibilities and relationships for each of us differ. You may not be a track star, but you run every day. You are to "run in such a way as to get the prize." You put on your shoes and head out to tackle the track or obstacle course of life. Most of our racetracks are not a single easy-to-navigate perfect circle. Rather, our responsibilities form this interconnected track. I can imagine some of the circles you may be running on right now:

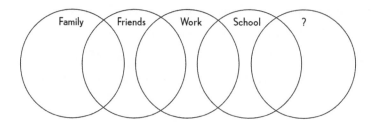

You can add others. You can fill in the question mark with something else you are involved in or responsible for. It makes for a rather complicated track, doesn't it?

We run at a faster pace because we have more things on our plates than ever before. We have glorious opportunities. We have incredible responsibilities. We have pressures. Life can get complicated when we do not know how to navigate one or more of the representational circles, but what a delight to enjoy so many different areas of life. Each one provides the opportunity to thrive if the circle is relationally driven. Of course there are tasks to be accomplished as well. Solomon's proverb helps us to keep the emphasis on righteousness that allows us to thrive:

Those who trust in their riches will F

A

L

L,

but the righteous will thrive like a green leaf.

Life's pace sometimes is quiet and profound—and not always dictated by us. "It is always the simple things that change our lives," writes Donald Miller in *Through Painted Deserts: Light, God, and Beauty on the Open Road*. "And these things never happen when you are looking for them to happen. Life will reveal answers at the pace life wishes to do so. You feel like running, but life is on a stroll. This is how God does things."

## PACE SHOULD BE BALANCED

As you study those circles of your life, you'll notice each well-paced area of responsibility in your life has a balance of three parts: a relational focus on God, a relational focus on others, and task completion.

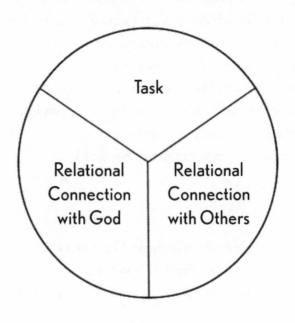

These three divisions of focus keep a relational emphasis while allowing you to accomplish needed tasks. For example, if you have an assignment at work, you need to fulfill that task. But you have a choice in how you do that. You can do the task with very little relational involvement, or you can connect in a respectful way with the people involved with that task. You can commit the task to God, asking for help to accomplish it well and in a God-glorifying way.

My laundry basket is currently overflowing. It is quite possible I may not have anything to wear tomorrow. I really need to do laundry. You get the idea. My four-year-old daughter loves to do laundry with me. It is much faster and easier if I do it alone. However, if I allow my four-year-old to participate in sorting the clothes, putting them in the washer, pouring in the soap, and closing the lid, I am completing the task while also building a relational connection with her. We're building a pace that thrives together.

At work, we had a staff meeting the day after Christmas. There were not many people in the office, and I was tasked with leading the meeting. It would have been easy to go through our list of responsibilities and be done. However, since it was a low staff day, it was a good time to keep the relational emphasis. I brought in cinnamon rolls and we ate together, completed our business together, and prayed together as a group. Doing this connected the three areas of task completion, relational connection with others, and relational connection with God.

If you are at home with family, perhaps the task is nurture or education. The relational connection with others may be easier here since the task is relational, but you still need to be intentional about the relational connection with God. It could involve praying for your family. Some days are a lot easier than others for getting dinner on the table. Thank God for the pizza delivery guy. Some days a noble accomplishment is just getting everyone to the table with clean hands. Getting the family to pause and pray for their food before devouring it can sometimes be a small miracle in and of itself. Maybe there are a few moments when you cook the food, order the food, pick up the food, set the table, or do the dishes that you could pray for each mouth in the family.

Life is often more interconnected and less defined than these circles suggest. They offer a basic way to think about trying to integrate a relational priority into your life. Balance usually does not work out like this perfectly divided pie chart. There are definitely times when the lines shift. A correct relational emphasis when we are tempted to focus on the mechanics or results of the task keeps us well paced.

## PACE REQUIRES REST

Balance allows us to set an endurable pace. Balance also gives us stability so that we are not easily knocked off our feet. You may have really good shoes for running and a good pace, but at some point you need to take off the shoes and rest. For most of us, rest is a hazy futuristic ambition. *Someday* I'll rest. But we need to build rest into our schedules to help us go the distance. You conserve oxygen when you slow down. This is good balance. Remember our previous discussion of the art of the *yes* and *no*. The Apostle Paul encouraged us: "Let us not become weary in doing good." Rest is, in essence, a recovery time for you physically, emotionally, and spiritually.

Building periods of rest into your schedule will help you thrive. Judaism has a system in place for balancing the pace of life with rest. The word *Shabbat*, which we translate as *Sabbath*, means "to cease." Sabbath is the practice of building in specific times to cease from doing all regular work. The idea of a Sabbath, a one day a week of rest, was not the norm in the ancient world. There was no such thing as a five- or six-day workweek. When you live off the land, the land has to be cared for every day, so everyone worked seven days a week from sunup to sundown. If you didn't work that day, you didn't eat. The Babylonian calendar had a few days when work stopped, but only because the date was believed to be evil, not because anyone was actually given rest.

But the ancient Jewish community worked six days and rested on the seventh. Their Sabbath observance was not only an exercise in rest but also one in trust that their Creator could provide for their seventh-day needs.

Today, most of us work a five-day, forty-hour workweek. Our American two-day weekend was developed in the 1920s as a means to accommodate both Jewish workers, who took Saturday as their Sabbath, *and* Christians, who took Sunday off as the day to celebrate Jesus' resurrection. As early as 1926, records indicate that Henry Ford shut down his Detroit automotive factories for all of Saturday and Sunday. In 1929 the Amalgamated Clothing Workers of America was the first union to demand and receive a five-day workweek. Slowly, other companies and industries followed their lead. By 1940 the two-day weekend had gained nationwide acceptance.

A Sabbath observance made God's top ten list, that is, the Ten Commandments. The expansive commandment even includes a precedent-reason: "In six days the LORD made the heavens and the earth, the sea, and all that is in them, but he rested on the seventh day. Therefore the LORD blessed the Sabbath day and made it holy." If God has time to take a break, don't we? The idea of breaking from your regular work to rest is mentioned thirty-five times in the Bible. I guess it was something that bears repeating.

Professor Norman Wirzba notes that *"the experience of delight is what the Sabbath is all about."* He encourages us to include corporate worship and family or group meals as part of our Sabbath rest, our pacing, emphasizing the relational aspects of showing "our joy and great pleasure in the gifts of God." What a righteous challenge—to take a regularly scheduled day or even a part of a day "to relish the goodness and beauty of God's work and to see in each other the trace of God."

## A PRACTICAL LOOK AT BALANCE

If you take one day a week as a Sabbath rest, is it possible to live a paced life the rest of the week? How do the hours add up?

Work is important. God calls us to work more than rest. Work makes us productive members of society. But some of us can get so caught up in our work that we forget that God gave us a rhythm, a pattern, a cycle designed to keep us healthy and sane. Have you ever neglected rest and then gotten sick and been forced to rest? It's a painful way to gain perspective on what is important in life. The balance of work and rest is part of the human design.

When we are out of balance with either too much work or too much play, our relationships suffer. Too much work means that we are likely not spending enough time with family and friends—if we have any left. We may need to reintroduce ourselves. When we do not work enough, well, our relationships suffer if we cannot pay the bills.

You have twenty-four hours today. (Remember those charts in chapter 5 to help you set goals?) You should sleep eight hours. I know that I do not thrive in terms of my tasks or relationships when I am tired. I get crabby. I am not creative or patient. When he was a baby, my second son timed it perfectly to be up for hours in the middle of the night and then settle down to sleep as his siblings woke up. Ah, those sleepless nights of parenting; they take their toll. But a priority to sleep to keep health and patience and feed creativity and right relationships is important.

That leaves sixteen waking hours. Let's say you eat three meals today. Perhaps you work an eight-hour shift. Exercise for an hour. That probably leaves you around five hours to spend with friends and family, shop for supplies, manage the household, keep records, play, worship, volunteer, and . . . Whew! If only we could stop time. Wouldn't that be great? Freeze it, or just slow it down?

There always seems to be more to do than time to do it. So how do you pace yourself to accomplish all that you need to do and enjoy the journey? It is a challenge to find the balance of reaching your potential and achieving all that God has in store for you. Living life to the fullest and enjoying it in abundance are worth finding your pace. Building in moments of renewal can make all the difference in your days.

Isaiah told us that

> those who hope in the LORD
>    will *renew* their strength.
> They will soar on wings like eagles;
>    they will run and not grow weary,
>    they will walk and not be faint.

King David prayed, "Create in me a pure heart, O God, / and *renew* a steadfast spirit within me." Prayer is a good place to seek God's leading for pace in your life. Prayer by its very nature often relaxes us as we pause to place our time in the hands of God. Prayer is an opportunity to commit our time to God. Martin Luther summed up his approach: "I have so much to do that I shall spend the first three hours in prayer." Ignatius of Loyola famously said, "We should pray as though everything depends on God . . . but we should work as though everything depended upon our efforts."

Opportunities for renewal often need to be created. Prayer. Rest. A vacation on a beach somewhere should fit the bill nicely for renewal. Wouldn't you agree? If we could only get away every time we needed our batteries recharged, would that be perfect? Until that well-deserved vacation on a distant beach rolls around, here are some ideas to get you rolling toward renewal.

Spend a few minutes each night as you lie down reflecting on how you spent your free time that day. Did it rejuvenate you? How about what you have done in the last week? What are some things that helped you feel energized? Where are some places that you can build those into your day tomorrow?

Give yourself minibreaks in the day to nourish your body. Have a snack. Drink extra water. Stretch. Rub your neck and upper shoulders to help your muscles relax, and have a break. Sit up straight and take deep breaths.

I know a prolific author who uses a timer. He makes a list of what he has to do and allots only a certain amount of time to it each day. He is a professor in addition to being a writer, so he must balance giving lectures, grading papers, doing research, meeting with students, attending meetings, and writing during his work hours. He sets his timer and writes every day for just an hour or two, whatever that day can hold. When the timer goes off, he closes down his computer and is finished with that until the next day. With such attention to his pace, he makes progress.

"Slow and steady wins the race" is the famous theme of one of Aesop's fables. The hare ridicules a slow-moving tortoise and challenges him to a race. The hare soon leaves the tortoise behind, confident he will win, and pauses to take a nap. As he awakens, the tortoise, his competitor, is finishing the race, having crawled slowly but steadily forward.

Even winning teams call time-outs to regroup and strategize. Call time-outs. Put them to good use so that you have the time to prioritize your day, your week, your month, and your life.

## PACING YOUR REACTION

Very few of us are born with patience. It is a skill that has to be developed. My dad learned patience by raising three daughters. It seems he was always waiting and waiting just to get my mom and his three girls out of the house! Even our dog was female. The man had bucketloads of patience.

Patience is listed in Galatians 5:22-24 as a fruit of the Spirit. That is, it is an attribute that God grows in us. Like a piece of actual fruit, the attribute of patience takes time to grow, ripen, and mature to harvest.

Luke told the story of Jesus traveling between Samaria and Galilee. It was a tense area interculturally. Jews and Samaritans did not spend time together. They didn't like each other at all. Jesus found himself on the outskirts of a village among people with leprosy. Leprosy was an incurable, contagious infection that caused major skin sores, disfigurement, and nerve damage. Anyone with leprosy was removed from the community.

The ten men with leprosy in this outcast community saw Jesus walking toward them, and they called out to him, "Jesus, have pity on us!" Jesus responded by telling them to go and be checked by the local priests for a clean bill of health. As they turned with hope in their hearts, they noticed their skin began to heal. As they moved forward, they were cured. Their lives were on the way to restoration.

Only one of the ten showed the patience and the strength of character to put his celebrations on hold for a moment, go back to where he found Jesus, and say thank you.

Having patience involves being slow to react, willing to wait. Patience involves our time management juxtaposed with relational investment. Often we are impatient when we aren't happy with how our time is being spent. Someone or some circumstance beyond our control is challenging our plans.

Patience helps us to slow our pace. It exercises self-control. Patience invests in the people more than the task. In *She Can Laugh at the Days to Come: Strengthening the Soul for the Journey Ahead*, Valerie Bell wrote,

> This is one of the encouraging evidences that God is active in my life. I am watching God grow me into having more patience with the people and situations to which I am not naturally inclined. Initially, I have my own perceptions. But just as God [has seen] past my rebellion to my hurt, I began to perceive more than what's on the surface.

## A SUPPORT SYSTEM IN PLACE

Who fills your cup? Who nourishes you? Who energizes you? Invest in those people who are crucial for your health and sanity. Find someone you look up to, and ask that person to mentor you. Let this person speak into your life and support you. Be willing to absorb the mentor's input as a means to help you grow.

Along with mentors, you need a few moments every day to hear that voice from heaven say, "Be still, and know that I am God." The Hebrew here is a strong command meaning "stop" or "halt."

God has all kinds of wonderful things for you in each season of life. Some seasons are much faster paced than others. But that pace is dangerous to maintain and not how you were created. Take time to rest and renew.

Other seasons are more slowly paced and provide wonderful opportunities to breathe easy. These are great times to practice moderation and be intentional about hearing from God. These seasons of rest prepare you for the next exhilaration. Pace yourself. Find balance. When you find moderation in life and have a pace that allows you to renew and refocus, you thrive. Thrive.

# DISCUSSION QUESTIONS

1. Do you feel as though you have a good balance in your life between work and rest?
2. Where do you think you need to make some changes?
3. How would you describe your pace in life?
4. What is your season in life right now?
5. Who do you know that seems to balance life well? What do you admire about them?
6. Write out what your life would look like if it were paced well and had good balance.
7. Write out practical ways you think you could achieve this balance and pace.

*Excellence is an art won by training and habituation: we do not act rightly because we have virtue or excellence, but we rather have these because we have acted rightly. . . . [We] are what we repeatedly do. Excellence, then, is not an act but a habit.*

—Will Durant

## CHAPTER 10

# SKELETON KEY

## *The Pursuit of Excellence*

GOD CREATED US SO INTRICATELY that even when nothing is left of us but bone, scientists can figure out a lot about us from those clues. Our skeletons leave keys to help them surmise what we ate, where we lived, injuries we sustained, hobbies we had . . . I broke my finger playing high school basketball. It ruined my future aspirations of being a hand model. To this day it is still crooked. That hobby, that injury, is set permanently in my bones.

There is also excellence down to our very bones in how God created us. When we repeat a skill, it's as though our bones remember it. We repeat a behavior again and again so that it is physically ingrained. If you play tennis, you have swung that tennis racket thousands of times. If you play basketball, you have shot thousands of baskets. Repetition often cements behaviors into the core of our being. That is part of how we learn. We do something again and again until it becomes a natural behavior. To learn something new, we must be taught. To thrive in life, we need to practice positive behaviors. We must repeat them until they become natural parts of our beings, all the way to our bones. Repetition leads to excellence.

## AN EXCELLENT WAY

If you know people who are thriving, I suspect you can name several things they do—or characteristics they exhibit—excellently. Michelangelo was an excellent painter who left his imprint on the Sistine Chapel. Abraham Lincoln was an excellent leader who united a divided country. Shakespeare was an excellent poet and playwright. Louis Armstrong was an excellent jazz musician. Isaac Newton was an excellent scientist. Michael Jordan was an excellent basketball player. The list goes on and on of people in history who catch our attention because they were not part of the ordinary masses. They excelled in a particular area.

Excellence is not plucked randomly out of the air. Achieving it requires effort: hard work, dedication, and self-control. There is a pursuit involved in living a healthy life, characterized by right relationships. Though the Bible often refers to righteousness as a fruit or gift, it is also described as something we should pursue. Paul told Timothy to "pursue righteousness, godliness, faith, love, endurance and gentleness," and "pursue righteousness, faith, love and peace . . . out of a pure heart." This pursuit is the invitation at your doorstep.

The often-quoted "love chapter" of the New Testament is introduced with Paul's bold sentence: "And yet I will show you the most *excellent* way." Excellence is a defining mark of a life lived well. Why is excellence important? Because you were made for it. You were made to reflect an excellent God. God has great joy when you do the things you were created to do.

The ancient Greeks had the concept of *aretē* (pronounced ar-e-tay), which means "virtue," "moral excellence," or "achieving the full potential." One way they highlighted this excellence was through sculpting the human body to be at peak physical condition and then creating an event to behold this greatness. The Olympics were born in Greece to feature outstanding physical performance. The tradition has stuck. We love to watch excellence. It is inspiring and awesome to behold someone who has trained hard with perseverance and dedication.

Life can be that way. Not just the Olympics. Not just sports. *Aretē* was a concept that embraced excellence with purpose. There was always a goal united with the desire. If your purpose is pure, excellence can benefit you and your whole community. You can change your world.

## EXCELLENT IN CHARACTER

Excellence, unfortunately, does not happen overnight. It is often a slow process. That is why so many people give up on its pursuit. We want dramatic results instantaneously, a huge reward for a little bit of effort. The momentary satisfaction of instant gratification is tough to beat. As difficult as it is, resist those schemes that promise reward without the work. Excellence is a lifestyle that sparkles like the diamond that has been painstakingly cut from the rock and then polished. The uncommon character trait of self-control is also rare and precious because it requires courage and commitment—one wise decision at a time. Whether it is saying no to a donut staring you in the face, a reality show calling your name, or the opportunity to spend money rather than save it, every choice you make defines who you are.

Remind yourself that you were made for excellence. Every day, say it out loud: "I am going to pursue excellence."

If an old pattern beckons you away from excellence, evaluate what triggers the temptation. When and where and with whom are you vulnerable? How can you build protective walls, boundaries, to create an environment that will allow you to succeed? Don't forget your emoticons.

Self-control not only builds character; it also communicates to others that you are trustworthy. If you can resist temptations, you are a friend, a parent, a spouse, a coworker who can be trusted. When you are faced with the opportunity to gratify self or remain true to the relationships in which you have invested, your choices reveal your loyalties. Self-control is a muscle of strength that can be exercised in difficult moments to preserve your relational integrity. As a person of self-control, you can preserve right relationships much more easily than a person given to self-gratification.

When Jesus was about to be arrested by soldiers, his friend and disciple Peter drew his sword and cut off the right ear of the high priest's servant. In a moment of passionate defense and terror, he defaulted to violence as a means to protect his rabbi. It was a moment of weakness, as we all have had.

It should have been fuel for the fire. The other disciples easily could have jumped on board and drawn their swords. An all-out sword fight could have ensued. Yet Jesus immediately calmed everyone. He showed self-control as the emotional and physical thermostat escalated. He de-escalated the situation. Jesus even righted the wrong by calmly bending down, picking up the amputated ear, and returning it to the man's head. It was a miracle that restored a man to wholeness, but it also modeled Jesus' self-control. Jesus' self-control helped to restore the relationships between him and his disciples and then between Jesus and the soldiers.

## EXCELLENT IN PURSUIT

I know that on some days, it is all we can do just to get by. It is impossible to be excellent at everything all the time. You can be excellent in the zone where God has placed you, whatever your profession and whatever your time is committed to. I know an excellent preschool teacher who is completely invested in teaching her four-year-olds their letters. She makes it fun. She has songs about letters, books about letters, hand motions about letters, and a letter bucket. Each week the kids can fill the letter bucket with things that start with the letter of the week. She is excellent at her job. She brings great joy to her students and their families because of her excellence.

I know an excellent grocery store. I have never loved a grocery store before. It has good parking. It takes my coupons. It has helpful store clerks, and they are kind to me. All their employees when they are in the aisles or stocking the shelves always stop and ask if I need help. It is friendly overload, a bit out of place in Los Angeles. The store has excellent customer service, and so I would much rather wait and grocery shop there than anywhere else. It has excellent management, excellent cashiers, and excellent baggers who offer to walk out in the pouring rain and load the car. Being in that store brings me joy. It spreads joy by its excellence.

What does excellence look like for you? What brings you the most joy? What would you like to spend more time doing? Set goals. Live out loud. When you live with excellence, not only does it bring you joy, but the joy overflows.

How do you become excellent at something? Invest in that subject. Become an avid learner. Study those who participate well in that area. Ask questions. Investigate others' methods. Adopt those practices for yourself. Read up on the subject. Fill your brain with excellent things: "Whatever is true, whatever is noble, whatever is right, whatever is pure, whatever is lovely, whatever is admirable—if anything is excellent [*aretē*] or praiseworthy—think about such things." Surrounding yourself with excellence (*aretē*) encourages you to pursue it. If you think about excellence, you are much more likely to achieve it.

It is amazing when you put the right thing in the right hands. A basketball in my hand is worth about $19. But if you put this same basketball in the hands of Kobe Bryant, it's suddenly worth $19 million a year. A golf ball and a club in my hands are worth about $100. In the hands of Tiger Woods they are worth $100 million. Give me a violin, and you'd probably pay money for me *not* to play it. But a violin in the hands of Joshua Bell is worth about $4 million. The value of something depends on whose hands it's in. When we are in God's hands and committed to the excellence for which God created us, whether it is basketballs, groceries, or letters, we will shine.

Civil rights leader Martin Luther King Jr. spoke about such excellence:

> If it falls your lot to be a street sweeper, sweep streets like Michelangelo painted pictures, like Shakespeare wrote poetry, like Beethoven composed music; sweep streets so well that all the host of Heaven and earth will have to pause and say, "Here lived a great street sweeper, who swept his job well."

## AN EXCELLENT END

There is a story of a friend of God, named Ezekiel, who was called to explain a bit about who God was and what God was up to throughout history. The story takes us to desert bones swirling with sand—hot, brittle, and forgotten. Ezekiel tells us that the eye of God does not miss a thing. Even in the midst of a desert sandstorm, God sees what others have forgotten. God does not overlook those bones peeking through that sea of sand. God seeks out those who are sunburned, parched, exhausted, and overlooked—and does incredible things.

God let Ezekiel see a remarkable sight. God picked up those bones lying in that desert valley and put flesh around them. As they began to again resemble human life, God gathered the winds from the far corners of the earth. From the north God called the wind. From the south God summoned the wind. From the east God harnessed the wind. And from the west God beckoned the wind. Those breezes had blown sand around those dry bones and buried them—death and despair.

But then God got hold of that wind and repurposed it. No longer was that wind haphazardly howling about the forsaken land. Now the four corners of the earth were harnessed by a powerful God who could restore life. God breathed life into those bones just as God breathed life into the first human. Ezekiel saw God transform despair into hope. He witnessed a God who took brokenness and restored it to wholeness. Those bones stood to their feet, and the flesh inhaled the oxygen that God breathed into the beings. God put his very spirit into them so that they could live an excellent life. God's real message to his people, through Ezekiel, was clear: "I will put my Spirit in you and you will live." Resurrection is life most excellently realized because it has defeated death!

My daughter has been running around the house lately and shouting, "Hey, Mom, God's got it!" I'm not sure where she picked that up, but I love it. I love to hear a four-year-old proclaiming that God's got what she doesn't. God's got what her mama doesn't. It could be the best thing ever for her to know. She has an excellent God who's got her back. Ezekiel saw God resurrect bones to life. Centuries later Jesus rose from the dead so that we would know *life*. We have a most excellent God who can restore dry bones and restore dry lives. This restoration is so that you can thrive with excellence.

"I will put my Spirit in you and you will live." What does that mean? It means I have excellent strength and excellent joy, and I embrace the truth of these words of Nehemiah: "The joy of the LORD is your strength." Excellence is not about putting pressure on you to be perfect. No one needs that burden. Excellence frees you to experience joy. In the movie *Chariots of Fire* Scottish track star Eric Liddell told his sister, "I believe God made me for a purpose, but He also made me fast. And when I run, I feel His pleasure." The race itself brought the thrill, the joy, to Liddell. Often there is a lot of repetition and practice of the same things in order to excel for game day. The persistence and perseverance of faithfully, righteously, fulfilling our *teleios* bring joy.

Booker T. Washington said that "excellence is to do a common thing in an uncommon way." Wally Amos was an air force veteran who loved cookies. He sent his home-baked chocolate chip cookies to celebrities to entice them to sign with his talent agency. In 1975 he took the advice of friends and opened a cookie store in Los Angeles and named it "Famous Amos." The first year he sold $300,000 worth of cookies. By 1982, his sales reached $12 million a year. Wally Amos was excellent in chocolate chip cookies and marketing.

Pursuing excellence does not mean you have to become famous or amass a fortune. Often those things can rob your joy. King Solomon warned against trusting in riches. Really, you can find excellence in just about anything you can imagine. Anything that is part of your life now can be done really well, even the small things. Sometimes those might even bring you the most joy. "If you cannot do great things, do small things in a great way," said Napoleon Hill.

To be excellent is to thrive. Proverbs 11:28 reminds us that to be excellent in life, to thrive, we learn to have excellent relationships in all that we do. Living with distinction and quality means that your relationships with others and your relationship with God are strong and healthy. Doing this will bring you joy and will help you thrive.

You have this one life. Really live. You were created to have this marvelous experience of being human, created in the image of God.

Behold the majestic oceans and sit by a quiet stream.

Watch an amazing sunset and find the Big Dipper.

Walk barefoot on a beach and sit by a crackling fire.

Memorize something inspirational.

Give to the poor.

Eat something strange.

Wear something funky.

Work.

Play.

Sleep.

Worship.

Fight for justice.

Dance.

Sing.

Pray.

Sweat.

Love.

Fast.

Cry.

Roll up your sleeves and get dirty.

Live.

Thrive.

Excellence, *aretē*, is the mark of a life that is thriving. I want you to thrive. God wants you to thrive.

This proverb tucked away and now rediscovered is full of potential for us. It is our wake-up call. It is our skeleton key. A skeleton key can open any lock. Finding something that works for everyone is pretty rare. Righteous living can work for anyone. This can be your key to a life that thrives.

Those who trust in their riches will F

A

L

L,

but the righteous will thrive like a green leaf.

This simple idea can change the way that you live. I would love for that to happen. Let me know when it does. I'd love to hear about your reading this book, taking it to heart, discovering ways to live excellently, sharing your heart of justice, living in right relationships. And thriving.

# DISCUSSION QUESTIONS

1. Who do you know who does something in an excellent way?
2. What makes it excellent?
3. In what area would you like to be excellent?
4. What do you think are some good steps to take to work toward excellence?
5. On a scale of one to ten, where would you rate your level of self-discipline?
6. What decisions can you make today that would help build that part of your character?
7. In what ways do you think you can invest in excellent relationships?
8. What steps do you plan to take to thrive in life?

# NOTES

1. BURIED TREASURE

*"Those who trust . . . green leaf."*
Proverbs 11:28 (emphasis added)
*The baby . . . was returned to her care.*
1 Kings 3:16-28
*People . . . hear Solomon's wisdom.*
1 Kings 10:24
*Even the famed Queen of Sheba . . . assess this wisdom.*
Queen Sheba was considered a queen regnant. That is a female monarch who reigns in her own right, in contrast to a queen consort, who is the wife of a reigning king.
*"The report I heard . . . was told me."*
1 Kings 10:6-7

*In writings . . . "There is nothing new under the sun."*

    Ecclesiastes 1:9

*When King Solomon shifted his focus . . . wealth, power, and status.*

    1 Kings 11

*"Oh, my love, my darling."*

    "Unchained Melody," originally recorded in 1965, became one of the most recorded songs of the twentieth century, spawning more than five hundred versions in hundreds of languages. It regained popularity when used in the 1990 film *Ghost*.

*"You've lost that lovin' feelin'."*

    "You've Lost That Lovin' Feelin'" was recorded in 1964 and became a number-one hit single in the United States and the United Kingdom in 1965.

*Jesus talked about . . . love God, love people.*

    Matthew 22:34-40; Mark 12:28-34; and Luke 10:25-28 record Jesus talking about the greatest commands.

*"Let perseverance finish its work . . . not lacking anything."*

    James 1:4

*Children are kidnapped . . . inexpensive chocolate.*

    *The Dark Side of Chocolate*, a documentary by Miki Mistrati and U. Roberto Romano, March 16, 2010.


## 2. "AYE, AYE, CAPTAIN"

*What comes out . . . reflects your heart.*

    Matthew 15:18

*Jesus put it this way, "All you need to say is simply 'Yes.'"*
Matthew 5:37

*Trust enables . . . righteousness that will thrive.*
Proverbs 11:28

## 3. C☺NSTRUCTI☹N & EM☹TIC☺NS

*Despite all the yeses of God . . . too tempting to resist.*
"The LORD God commanded the man, 'You are free to eat from any tree in the garden; but you must not eat from the tree of the knowledge of good and evil, for when you eat from it you will certainly die.'" (Genesis 2:16-17)

*"It had been my general practice . . . weakened me as a Christian."*
John Woolman, *The Journal of John Woolman and a Plea for the Poor* (Secaucus, N.J.: Citadel, 1972), 41, cited in Richard Foster, *Money, Sex, and Power* (San Francisco: HarperCollins, 1985), 67.

*We may not know the mind of God . . .*
"Oh, the depth of the riches of the wisdom and knowledge of God! How unsearchable his judgments, and his paths beyond tracing out!

'Who has known the mind of the Lord?'"
(Romans 11:33-34)

*but we do know the heart of God.*
"For God so loved the world that he gave his one and only Son, that whoever believes in him shall not perish but have eternal

life. For God did not send his Son into the world to condemn the world, but to save the world through him." (John 3:16-17)

*"Having clear boundaries . . . limits and limitations."*

Henry Cloud and John Townsend, *Boundaries* (Grand Rapids: Zondervan, 1992).

*Author and nationally syndicated radio show host . . . establish priorities.*

Through a plan known as Financial Peace University, Dave Ramsey's organization teaches about managing finances and getting rid of debt.

*It is much easier for people . . . "speaking the truth in love."*

Ephesians 4:15

*"the righteous will thrive"*

Proverbs 11:28

*Thomas Edison . . . "If I find 10,000 ways . . . step forward."*

As quoted in an ad for GPU Nuclear Corporation, in *Black Enterprise*, vol. 16, no. 11 (June 1986): 79. Edison commented that "many of life's failures are people who did not realize how close they were to success when they gave up" (this is presented as a statement of 1877, as quoted in *From Telegraph to Light Bulb with Thomas Edison* by Deborah Hedstrom-Page [Nashville: B&H Publishing, 2007], 22).

A Time to Kill *was . . . 275 million copies.*

Information from www.jgrisham.com/bio/ and *CBS This Morning*, April 11, 2012, www.cbsnews.com/8301-505263_162-57412275/john-grisham-e-books-will-be-half-of-my-sales/.

*"It is essential . . . called 'common sense.' "*

Hannah Whitall Smith, *The Christian's Secret of a Happy Life*,
new and enlarged ed. (New York: Fleming H. Revell, 1888),
97.

*As Jesus declared, "All you need . . . 'Yes' or 'No.'"*

Matthew 5:37

## 4. SPLINTERS

*Jesus asked poignant questions . . . "Why do you . . . your own
eye."*

Matthew 7:3-4

*He said, "If you forgive . . . will not forgive your sins."*

Matthew 6:14-15

*"The righteous will thrive."*

Proverbs 11:28

*Carpentry was the family business.*

"Isn't this the carpenter's son?" (Matthew 13:55)

*Jesus was like no one they had ever known.*

See Mark 2:1-12; Matthew 9:2-6.

*"Father, forgive them . . . do not know what they are doing."*

Luke 23:34

*Being forgiven . . . amazing experience.*

"In him we have redemption through his blood, the forgiveness
of sins, in accordance with the riches of God's grace" (Ephesians
1:7). See also Acts 10:43; 13:38 and Colossians 1:13-14.

*The Bible says . . . remembers it no more.*

    Psalm 103:12-16

*God loves the world . . . relationally.*

    John 3:16-17

*"If anyone is in Christ . . . the righteousness of God."*

    2 Corinthians 5:17-21

*When a disciple asked Jesus . . . that number by seventy.*

    Matthew 18:21-22

*Jesus invites us to forgive . . . be forgiven often.*

    Luke 6:37

*Jesus wants us to be a people . . . forgive one another.*

    "I you forgive other people when they sin against you, your heavenly Father will also forgive you. But if you do not forgive others their sins, your Father will not forgive your sins." (Matthew 6:14-15)

*To thrive, we reach . . . extend forgiveness.*

    "Bear with each other and forgive whatever grievances you may have against one another. Forgive as the Lord forgave you." (Colossians 3:13)

*"No. I distinctly remember forgetting it."*

    See Luis Palau, *Experiencing God's Forgiveness* (Portland, OR: Multnomah, 1984), 19.

# 5. LIVE OUT LOUD

*"The righteous will thrive."*

    Proverbs 11:28

*Another proverb of Solomon reads, "Commit . . . your plans."*

Proverbs 16:3

*"The plans of the diligent . . . " as another proverb relates.*

Proverbs 21:5

*We are to "press on . . . win the prize."*

"Brothers and sisters, I do not consider myself yet to have taken hold of it. But one thing I do: Forgetting what is behind and straining toward what is ahead, I press on toward the goal to win the prize for which God has called me heavenward in Christ Jesus." (Philippians 3:13-14)

*There is a long history . . . wishes up to heaven.*

The planet Venus is named for the Roman goddess of love and is always the brightest point in the sky. The Romans built temples to Venus, and since it was the first "star" that could be seen in the sky for much of the year, and always the brightest whether seen in the morning or the evening, it was easy to remember it as a prayer point.

## 6. DRAGON SLAYING

*Jesus told his listeners . . . "enough trouble of its own."*

Matthew 6:34

*The Apostle Paul encouraged . . . "whatever is true . . . such things."*

Philippians 4:8

*"Behold the turtle . . . sticks its neck out."*

    James G. Hershberg, *James B. Conant: Harvard to Hiroshima and the Making of the Nuclear Age* (Stanford: Stanford University Press, 1993), 89.

*"You will know the truth . . . set you free."*

    John 8:32

*"So do not fear, for I am with you . . . righteous right hand."*

    Isaiah 41:10

*"Courage is doing what . . . unless you're scared."*

    Quoted in *Eddie Rickenbacker: An American Hero in the Twentieth Century* by David Lewis (Baltimore: Johns Hopkins University Press, 2005), 124.

*When you are in a panic . . . "the righteous are as bold as a lion."*

    Proverbs 28:1

*Take every thought captive . . . control you*

    2 Corinthians 10:5

*The Apostle Paul mentioned . . . "God exalted him [Jesus] . . . glory of God the Father."*

    Philippians 2:9-11 (emphasis added)

*Remind yourself of Jesus' promise: "Come to me . . . give you rest."*

    Matthew 11:28

*To help the young man . . . appropriate heartfelt trust.*

    See Judson Cornwall, *Praying the Scriptures* (Lake Mary, FL: Creation House, 1990), 52–54.

*When Roosevelt faced . . . four "essential human freedoms,"*

    Eric Foner, *The Story of American Freedom* (New York: W. W. Norton, 1999), 223.

*Rosa said, "I have learned over the years . . . does away with fear."*

Rosa Parks with Gregory J. Reed, *Quiet Strength: The Faith, the Hope, and the Heart of a Woman Who Changed a Nation* (Grand Rapids: Zondervan, 2000), 17.

*Shalom is a common Jewish greeting . . . "grace and peace."*

Paul picked up on this idea when he used the Greek term *eirēnē* for "peace" in Romans 5:1: "Therefore, since we have been justified through faith, we have peace with God through our Lord Jesus Christ."

## 7. SWAT

*A whole swarm of attitudes and behaviors . . . changed.*

"Get rid of all moral filth and the evil that is so prevalent and humbly accept the word planted in you, which can save you." (James 1:21)

*George Washington Carver offered these words of wisdom: "How . . . all of these."*

George Washington Carver, U.S. Department of the Interior, National Park Service, George Washington Carver National Monument, at www.nps.gov/nr/travel/cultural_diversity/G_Washington_Carver_Historic_Site.html.

*"The righteous will thrive."*

Proverbs 11:28

*God has always had a heart . . . taken advantage of.*

"The LORD your God is God of gods and Lord of lords, the great God, mighty and awesome, who shows no partiality and accepts no bribes. He defends the cause of the fatherless and the widow, and loves the alien, giving him food and clothing." (Deuteronomy 10:17-18)

*Rabbi Nancy Fuchs-Kreimer . . . "widows and orphans . . . fields of Boaz."*

Nancy Fuchs-Kreimer, "A Jewish Exploration: Widows, Orphans, and Charity-as-Justice," *Cathedral Age* (Fall 2006), 18.

*An estimated . . . trafficked into slavery.*

Quentin Hardy, "Global Slavery, by the Numbers," on *New York Times*, March 6, 2013, http://bits.blogs.nytimes.com/2013/03/06/global-slavery-by-the-numbers/.

*According to the Bible, Jesus fed five thousand . . . one sitting.*

The Feeding of the Five Thousand is one of the only miracles recorded in all four Gospels: Matthew 14:13-21; Mark 6:30-44; Luke 9:10-17; John 6:1-14.

*But the Bible tells us . . . "He has shown . . . humbly with your God."*

Micah 6:8

*Jo Anne tells the story . . . "When we . . .blessing of purpose."*

Jo Anne Lyon, *The Ultimate Blessing* (Indianapolis: Wesleyan Publishing House, 2003), 103–4.

*"Do not exploit . . . in court."*

Proverbs 22:22

*He and Christian friends . . . "ended up expending . . . good is all about."*

Steve Monsma, *Healing for a Broken World: Christian Perspectives on Public Policy* (Wheaton, IL: Crossway, 2008), 56.

Gregg A. *Ten Elshof points out . . . "a realistic sense . . . other goods."*

Gregg A. Ten Elshof, *I Told Me So: Self-Deception and the Christian Life* (Grand Rapids: Eerdmans, 2009), 117.


## 8. RANDOM RAINBOWS

*After an unparalleled storm . . . as a promise.*

The story of the Flood is found in Genesis 6–9.

*It is a belief that God holds it all together.*

"By him all things were created: things in heaven and on earth, visible and invisible, whether thrones or powers or rulers or authorities; all things were created by him and for him. He is before all things, and in him all things hold together." (Colossians 1:16-17)

*The God of hope . . . "fill you with all joy and peace . . . the Holy Spirit."*

Romans 15:13

*Euripides even called it "man's curse."*

From *The Suppliants* in *The Plays of Euripides*, trans. Edward P. Coleridge, vol. 1 (London: George Bell & Sons, 1891), 201.

*Jeremiah recorded: "'I know the plans . . . hope and a future.'"*

Jeremiah 29:11

*The thrive master . . . "I have come that they . . . have it to the full [thrive]."*

John 10:10

*Arthur Gordon . . . "the Easter story . . . this planet."*

Arthur Gordon, *A Song Called Hope* (Norwalk, CT: C. R. Gibson, 1985), 40.

*Learn from it. Live. Thrive.*

This story is found in John 8:1-12.

*"Everything that was written in the past . . . have hope" . . . find hope.*

Romans 15:4

*Hope is so essential . . . define us human beings.*

"May the God of hope fill you with all joy and peace as you trust in him, so that you may overflow with hope by the power of the Holy Spirit." (Romans 15:13)

*In the Bible . . . faith and love.*

"And now these three remain: faith, hope and love. But the greatest of these is love" (1 Corinthians 13:13). See also Colossians 1:5; 1 Thessalonians 1:3; 5:8.

*"Faith goes up the stairs that love has made . . . hope has opened."*

Attributed to Charles Spurgeon.

*"Hope rests on faith, love on hope, and victory on love."*

Nicholas of Flüe, quoted in *The Wisdom of the Saints*, ed. Jill Haak Adels (New York: Oxford University Press, 1987), 49.

*Faith asks for confidence . . . other than ourselves.*

"Know that a [person] is not justified by observing the law, but by faith in Jesus Christ. So we, too, have put our faith in Christ Jesus that we may be justified by faith in Christ and not by observing the law, because by observing the law no one will be justified." (Galatians 2:16)

*American clergyman . . . "God puts . . . is despondent."*

Henry Ward Beecher, *Life Thoughts* (New York: Sheldon and Co., 1860), 131.

*"When I left their house . . . slats and a sturdy headboard."*

Joy Jordan-Lake, *Why Jesus Makes Me Nervous* (Brewster, MA: Paraclete, 2007), 134–35.

*Hope is vital . . . "We who have fled . . . firm and secure."*

Hebrews 6:18-19

*Moses urged the people of Israel, "This day . . . the* LORD *is your life."*

Deuteronomy 30:19-20

*"When we are stuck . . . the task seems impossible."*

Leslie Williams, *When Women Build the Kingdom* (New York: Crossroad, 2006), 112–13.

## 9. DON'T WASTE OXYGEN

*You are to "run . . . get the prize?"*

1 Corinthians 9:24

*"Those who trust in their riches will fall."*

Proverbs 11:28

*"It is always the simple things . . . how God does things"*

Donald Miller, *Through Painted Deserts: Light, God, and Beauty on the Open Road* (Nashville: Thomas Nelson, 2005).

*The Apostle Paul . . . "Let us not become weary in doing good."*

Galatians 6:9

*Our American two-day weekend . . . Jesus' resurrection.*

"A Weekend History Lesson," *Weekend America*, American Public Radio, November 24, 2007, http://weekendamerica. publicradio.org/display/web/2007/11/24/a_weekend_history_ lesson.

*As early as 1926, records indicate that Henry Ford . . . Sunday.*

Douglas Brinkley, "The 40-Hour Revolution," *Time*, March 31, 2003.

*In 1929 the Amalgamated Clothing Workers . . . followed their lead.*

Alan Colmes, *Thank the Liberals\*: \*For Saving America* (Carlsbad, CA: Hay House, 2012), 40.

*By 1940 the two-day weekend . . . nationwide acceptance.*

Katherine Lawrence, *Labor Legislation* (New York: Rosen Publishing Group, 2006). "In 1940, the maximum number of hours that had to be worked was changed to forty each week. . . . In 1942, the Fair Labor Standards Act was modified. . . . The five-day workweek followed by a two-day weekend was required for all affected businesses" (25).

*"In six days the LORD made . . . it holy."*

Exodus 20:8-11

*Professor Norman Wirzba notes . . . "to relish the goodness . . . trace of God."*

Norman Wirzba, *Living the Sabbath* (Grand Rapids: Brazos, 2006), 52–53.

*Isaiah told us that "those who hope in the LORD . . . not be faint."*

Isaiah 40:31 (emphasis added)

*King David prayed, "Create in me . . . steadfast spirit within me."*

Psalm 51:10 (emphasis added)

*Martin Luther summed up . . . "I have so much . . . three hours in prayer."*

Edward McKendree Bounds, *Purpose in Prayer* (New York: Fleming H. Revell, 1920), 31.

*Ignatius of Loyola famously said, "We should pray . . . our efforts."*

Norbertine Fathers, *Annals of Saint Joseph*, vols. 34–36 (West De Pere, WI: Norbertine Fathers, 1922), 443.

*Only one of the ten showed the patience . . . and say thank you.*

See Luke 17:11-17.

*"This is one of the encouraging evidences . . . what's on the surface."*

Valerie Bell, *She Can Laugh at the Days to Come: Strengthening the Soul for the Journey Ahead* (Grand Rapids: Zondervan, 1996), 97.

*Along with mentors . . . "Be still, and know that I am God."*

Psalm 46:10

## 10. SKELETON KEY

*"Pursue righteousness, godliness, faith, love . . . gentleness."*

1 Timothy 6:11

*"Pursue righteousness, faith, love and peace . . . pure heart."*

2 Timothy 2:22

*The often-quoted "love chapter" . . . "And yet . . . most* excellent *way."*

1 Corinthians 12:31 (emphasis added)

*You were made to reflect an excellent God.*

"His divine power has given us everything we need for life and godliness through our knowledge of him who called us by his own glory and goodness. Through these he has given us his very great and precious promises, so that through them you may participate in the divine nature and escape the corruption in the world caused by evil desires." (2 Peter 1:3-4)

*Jesus' self-control helped to restore . . . Jesus and the soldiers.*

See Luke 22:50-51.

*She is excellent at her job.*

Thank you, Rebekah Mehany at Western Christian Preschool!

*It has excellent management . . . load the car.*

Shout out to Claremont Vons on Baseline and Mills!

*"Whatever is true, whatever is noble . . . such things."*

Philippians 4:8

*"If it falls your lot to be a street sweeper . . . swept his job well."*

Martin Luther King Jr., *A Testament of Hope: The Essential Writings and Speeches of Martin Luther King, Jr.*, ed. James M. Washington (New York: HarperCollins, 1986), 139.

*God's real message . . . "I will put my Spirit in you and you will live."*

Ezekiel 37:14

*It means . . . "The joy of the* LORD *is your strength."*

Nehemiah 8:10

*In the movie* Chariots of Fire . . . *"I believe God made me . . . His pleasure."*

Colin Welland, *Chariots of Fire*, directed by Hugh Hudson (Allied Stars Ltd., 1981), http://imdb.com/character/ch0016125/quotes.

*Booker . . . "excellence is to do a common thing in an uncommon way."*

"Booker T. Washington," on Biography.com, http://biography.com/people/booker-t-washington-9524663.

*Wally Amos . . . chocolate chip cookies and marketing.*

"Famous Amos Chocolate Chip Cookie Company," *Encyclopedia of Business*, 2nd ed., http://referenceforbusiness.com/businesses/A-F/Famous-Amos-Chocolate-Chip-Cookie-Company.html.

*"Those who trust in their riches . . . green leaf."*

Proverbs 11:28

CPSIA information can be obtained
at www.ICGtesting.com
Printed in the USA
FSHW02n0816230518
48555FS